The Great Revelation

Colin Urquhart

Every blessing,

Colin Urquhart

Gal 2:20.

Published by Integrity Media Europe, Unit 1 Hargreaves Business Park, Hargreaves Road, Eastbourne, East Sussex BN23 6QW

Cover design: Jon Smethurst, Ezekiel Design
Set in Garamond 11.5/14pt
Typeset by Helen Hancox

ISBN 978-1-907080-00-5

The Great Revelation

Colin Urquhart

For all who wish to live the lives Jesus Christ has made possible for us, through His great love for us.

ACKNOWLEDGEMENTS

I want to express my thanks to the Lord for the way He has taught me the principles of scripture that are truly 'The Great Revelation' that has been the foundation of my life and ministry.

I am also thankful for all those believers with whom these truths are lived out, especially all those who are part of Kingdom Faith.

My thanks also to Karen Rodrigues for the many hours of word processing and editing. She has been a great encouragement.

I am so blessed by my wife, Caroline, and my wonderful family, all of whom have Christ in them. We are united in our love for one another, and in His love for us all.

New Testament quotations from *THE TRUTH, the New Testament easily understood*, by Colin Urquhart, published by Integrity, June 2009. See Appendix 2 for further information about this new version..

CONTENTS

CHAPTER 1

REVELATION OF THE TRUTH

There are two great truths that determine the way every Christian is intended to live. The first of these speaks of the position that the believer has in Christ. When born again, he or she is incorporated into Christ and is then able to share in His life and inheritance completely. Paul tells the Colossians:

> 'Because you died with Christ, your life is now hidden with Christ – in God!' (Col. 3:3)

The second truth is complementary to this: Paul also speaks of,

> 'the glorious riches that are centred in this mystery that Christ has now come to live in you and in Him alone is your hope of glory, now and for all eternity.' (Col. 1:27)

So here are the two great truths about you as a Christian believer: you live in Christ and Christ lives in you. This, of course, is the outworking of the command that Jesus gave His disciples at the last supper:

> 'Stay living in Me and I will continue to live in you.' (John 15:4)

Literally this means: 'Continue to live in me and I continue to live in you.' Of course, you can only continue to live in Christ because this is where God has placed you already! It is the result of His wonderful grace that Christ continues to live in you. And it is this latter truth that we will concentrate on in this book.

What does it mean to say that because you live in Christ, He continues to live in you? How can we understand such amazing statements from God's

Word? How can Christ be reigning in glory in heaven, and yet be living in every true believer in Him? And what practical impact will this truth have on our daily lives?

If Christ lives in a person, His intention is to have a serious and dynamic impact on his or her life! We shall see that this is the key to living a victorious Christian life, which is God's purpose for every believer. Paul writes:

> 'But thanks be to God, for He always leads us in His trium-
> phant procession because we are in Christ. And He uses us
> everywhere we go to spread the truth about Him. For we
> are to God like the perfume of Christ among those who are
> being saved; the sweet fragrance of life.' (2 Cor. 2:14)

When the Holy Spirit writes to the seven churches in Asia Minor in Revelation chapters 2 and 3, every one of those churches are reminded that those who receive the wonderful promises about heaven are those who overcome, who conquer or who are victorious!

Yet it seems that for many the Christian life is a struggle and such victory is elusive. Is it really possible in this day and age to overcome whatever comes against us? We shall see this is not an unattainable ideal, but the practical way in which God has made it possible for us to live.

> 'It is immediately obvious that you can often fail, but the
> Christ in you cannot fail! Nothing is able to overcome
> Him! As Jesus Himself said: "When you believe, everything
> becomes possible!"' (Mark 9:23)

I want to guide you through a series of scriptural truths that will enable you to receive fresh revelation that Christ lives in you and that will show how this great truth will have practical consequences for you, taking you to a place of victory! **This is not empty triumphalism, but the way in which God intends you to live because of all He has accomplished for you in His Son, Jesus Christ!**

CHAPTER 2

CHRIST LIVES IN ME

The great apostle Paul lived and taught the churches this great truth from his own practical experience. He summarises his personal testimony in one key verse:

> *'I have been crucified together with Christ; the person I was no longer lives, but Christ now lives in me. The life I live in my body I live by faith in God's Son who has loved me by giving Himself on my behalf.' (Gal. 2:20)*

We will begin by looking at this verse phrase by phrase.

'I have been crucified together with Christ'

At the time of the crucifixion Paul (or Saul of Tarsus as he was known then) was definitely an enemy of Jesus Christ. He persecuted the church at first, utterly convinced that he was serving his God by so doing, intent on maintaining the traditions of his Jewish faith.

His encounter with the risen Christ on the way to persecute the church in Damascus, radically altered his life and perception of Jesus. He came to realise that he was actually involved personally in the event of the crucifixion!

Jesus not only took the sins of the whole of humanity upon Himself when He went to the cross, He took every sinner with Him. Here was the Innocent One dying on behalf of the guilty, the Holy One giving His life for the unholy, the Sinless One dying for sinners, the One who was totally acceptable in God's sight making His life a sacrifice on behalf of those who lived under condemnation because of their guilt.

Jesus offered the one, perfect sacrifice that would satisfy God's right judgment on those who sin: that they deserve to die and be eternally separated from Him. In His great love, He did not want humanity to be condemned to such judgment. So Jesus suffered the punishment we deserve!

This is why it was necessary for Him, though not guilty, to die the death of a condemned criminal by being crucified. In saying that He died for us, it would not have been enough for someone to assassinate Him by running a sword through Him. He had to die the death of a condemned sinner, although He had never sinned Himself!

Saul of Tarsus regarded himself as a righteous Pharisee, the strictest and most religious party within Judaism. He was intent on serving his God faithfully. He came to realise that he had been proud and self-righteous in thinking that he could become acceptable to God through his own religious activities, even though he was so strict in his religious observances. Instead, he embraced the gospel, the good news of Jesus Christ:

> *'We teach clearly that there is no other way for a person to be saved from his or her sins and the eternal condemnation he or she deserves. Faith in Jesus is the only way of salvation, and this has nothing to do with God's law. It is clear, then, that He is God not only of the Jews but of anyone of any nation who puts his faith in Jesus.' (Rom. 3:21-22)*

To be made righteous in God's sight is to become totally acceptable to Him. Instead of being sinners worthy only of judgment, condemnation and eternal separation from Him, we become those who are totally forgiven, completely acceptable to Him and made one with Him.

This was the amazing revelation that changed Paul's life. He realised that there was nothing he could do to please God or make himself acceptable in His sight. He did not even have to try to do this, for God had already done in His Son everything that was necessary to make him acceptable in God's eyes. Why try to accomplish what was already done? He merely needed to believe what God had done for him in Christ.

And so it has been for every sinner throughout the history of the church. No amount of religious activity, of church-going or spiritual discipline, could ever make us acceptable or worthy of salvation. That salvation which restores us to a relationship with God could only be accomplished by God Himself. And this He has done through the cross.

So Paul came to realise that when He went to the cross Jesus took Saul of Tarsus with Him; not only his sin, but the sinner. There Saul died when Christ died, so that when he had put his faith in Him, Christ's risen life would become his life.

> *'It is our love for Christ that compels us to action. We are convinced that He died for all and therefore all have died with Him. But if He died for all it means that those of us who have received His risen life should no longer live for ourselves, but for the One who died and was raised again for us!*
>
> *So from this point onwards we will not assess anyone by worldly standards. We used to have a very worldly view of Christ, but that is no longer the case. Now we are sure that if anyone is in Christ, made one with Him by their faith in Him, then that person is a new creation. The old person he was has died, is buried and finished with – gone forever. Now he has become a new person.' (2 Cor. 5:14-17)*

So when Jesus Christ went to the cross, He not only took Saul of Tarsus, He took the sinner you used to be. **You were crucified with Christ also. The sinner you used to be no longer lives, but now Christ lives in you!**

'The person I was no longer lives'

Death means the end of a life. Paul did not doubt that when he put his faith in what Jesus Christ had done for him on the cross, that the life he had lived formerly was dead, buried and finished with. All his attempts at pleasing God with his religious fervour had proved futile and unnecessary. If total acceptance was available through believing what Christ had done for him, why try to make himself acceptable? What God had done in His Son was perfect, and it is not possible to improve on the perfect! **So he could humbly** and truthfully accept and receive as a gift from God, the salvation that Jesus Christ had made possible on the cross.

Paul came to understand that the significance of being baptised in water as a believer was to signify the end of his former life and the beginning of an entirely new life. It was the funeral service of his old life. **Now he could enjoy a life lived in union with Christ: living in Christ and Christ living in him!**

So, too, for you. Your baptism as a believer was the funeral service for your old life. **Now you are a new creation and Christ has come to live in you in the person of His Spirit.** This signals the beginning of a radical new life-style for you, as it did for Paul.

Why is this not always apparent for Christians today? Because not every Christian believes he or she no longer lives, that the old has gone and the new has come. It is not possible to live fully in your new life if you still see yourself as the same person you used to be before you came to know Jesus Christ personally!

Like Paul, you need to speak the truth about yourself: '**I have been cruci-fied with Christ and I no longer live. Therefore I do not need to think of myself as the sinful failure I used to be. Now I can see myself as a new person with Christ living in me!**'

'But Christ now lives in me'

This truth made Paul a new man, a different person. It is this truth that makes you a different man or woman from the person you used to be!

Paul does not say that a blessing from Christ lives in him, but Christ Himself lives in him. This is a radical truth with far-reaching consequences. He has the life of Christ Himself within him.

As with you! You were crucified with Christ. **The person you used to be no longer lives, but now you are a new person with Jesus Christ living in you! The One who is reigning victorious in heaven also lives in you in the fullness of who He is.** This is the life Jesus said He came to make possible for all who believe in Him.

> '*The thief's purpose is to steal, kill and destroy. That is what the devil is like. But I have come to give the fullness of God's life to those who believe in Me.*' (John 10:10)

The full life of God, eternal life, Christ in you! Not at some time in the future but *now*! You have His life at this present time. If you have been born again Christ already lives in you!

This truth will not have impacted your life in the way God intended if you do not believe that Christ is in you, if you still see yourself as the same person you used to be, or if you still trust in yourself instead of trusting in Him. Why should this prove to be difficult for some believers to understand?

The secret is in realising that the strength, the power and victory belong to the Christ in you, and not to yourself. We shall see later that you remain weak as a human being, but your weakness does not matter if Christ is in you. In fact, your weakness can be an advantage, for it can encourage you to put your trust in the Christ who lives within you, instead of trusting in yourself! You are certainly a new creation, but you are still a weak human being compared with the might and power of Christ!

So we have to learn to trust in Him instead of ourselves, so that His life in us is expressed in every situation in which we are placed. This is a matter of faith and knowing how to apply that faith.

'The life I now live in my body, I live by faith in God's Son'

The Christian life is a matter of faith from start to finish. Paul had to learn that he needed to trust in the Christ within him, and not himself. And each one of us needs to do likewise.

I have learned to thank God when I fail. Does that seem strange? Well, I have come to understand that I only fail when I trust in myself and neglect or ignore the presence of Christ within me. When I trust in Him, He succeeds! **This is the key to successful living: not to trust in yourself, even in your strong abilities, but to stand to one side so the Christ in you can express His life through you.** We will see how to do this in practice!

Throughout every day you have this choice before you: to trust in yourself or in Christ who lives in you. The choice you make will have a dramatic effect on the outcome! **What amazing love that Christ should have come to live in you so that He can now be your life!**

'Who has loved me by giving himself on my behalf'

Paul places this phrase in the historic tense, 'He has loved me'! Jesus Christ had already proved His love for him and for all mankind by giving His life as a sacrifice to the Father on our behalf. Now all our sins can be forgiven, we can be made totally acceptable to God and His Son can come to live in us.

Potentially these great truths are possible for anyone who takes Jesus Christ to be his or her personal Lord and Saviour. **Nobody need question again whether God loves him or her. The matter is already settled beyond dispute. God has shown His love for us. He has demonstrated and proved this love beyond question.**

Jesus warned His disciples that in this world they would have great troubles. People had hated Him; they would hate them. They had rejected and persecuted Him; they would do the same to His followers.

So having Christ in him did not make Paul immune from such trouble. But he had the living Christ within him to enable him to persevere and emerge victorious from whatever difficulties were thrown against him.

> *'We have known times of glory and yet have been treated with dishonour. Sometimes we have been praised, at other times we have been slandered. Although we are genuine we have been regarded by some as impostors. Sometimes we are well known, in other places nobody knows who we are. We had been close to death, but we are still here! We have been beaten, but not killed. Even in times of sorrow we have continued to rejoice. Even when poor ourselves, we have been able to make many rich through what they have received from God. We have nothing ourselves, yet truly we have everything in Christ!' (2 Cor. 6:8-10)*

The same is true for you. The world is still the world. **You are still weak in yourself, but you have Christ within you to be your life, your strength, your victory over every adversity.** It is a matter of knowing how to live in the good of these glorious truths. The life of faith allows the Christ in you to face the difficulties and to overcome, without you struggling with your own human weakness to be victorious.

Before we see how to do this, we need to appreciate what it really means to say that Christ lives in us and has now become our life. To do this we will turn to another key verse of revelation.

CHAPTER 3

CHRIST, OUR WISDOM
FROM GOD

We have seen that we were placed in Christ by God's gracious act. Now we can see the wonderful consequence of this:

> *'It is only through God's own work of grace that you now live in Christ Jesus, at one with Him. Jesus Himself has become, for us who believe, the true wisdom that God has supplied. He is our righteousness. He is our holiness. He is our redemption, the one who has made it possible for us to be God's children.'* (1 Cor. 1:30)

God is true Wisdom. In the Old Testament He gave His people Israel the written law by which they were to live. He had given them a series of wonderful promises within the covenant He made with them. Under the terms of this covenant, the terms of their relationship with Him, He would be their God and they would be His people. The promises He gave them would be fulfilled if they were obedient in obeying the Law He gave them.

Time and time again they failed to do this. At times they sought to obey Him, but failed. At other times they turned away from their God in rebellion and even lost sight of the Law altogether.

But throughout the writings of the Law and the Prophets, God was looking forward to another time when He would do something completely new that would empower His people to live in obedience to His will and to inherit what He had promised them.

The period when Israel lived under the Law demonstrated that people could not please Him by their own efforts. No matter how hard they tried they could not live in righteousness, in ways that were right in God's sight and that pleased Him.

So where is God's wisdom in this? He had to prove to mankind that there was no way in which he could save himself from sin and failure. He could not live up to God's standard by depending on his own ability, no matter how determined he was, or how hard he tried. Even when he wanted to please God, he always failed to do so because of his sinful nature. He wanted to please himself rather than God. He wanted to use God to meet his needs, but did not want to obey God, especially if this proved costly.

This self-life in the New Testament is called 'the flesh.' Jesus said that it is the Spirit who gives you life. Your natural life counts for nothing. (John 6:63) Most Christians do not truly believe this. They try to change themselves to be more like Jesus, thinking that this is a godly thing to do, whereas it is impossible and a denial of the good news of what God has accomplished in His Son, Jesus Christ.

He was not sent by the Father to change us, for He knew that to be impossible. **He was sent to exchange His life for us. We were to be crucified with Him, not subjected to a course of improvement. We were to be made new, not better! That natural sinful life was to be put to death and replaced by a new life – Christ in us, the hope of glory, now and for all eternity.** (Col. 1:27).

The reason why so many Christians appear to fail is that they pray to be changed instead of realising that Christ Himself has now become their new life. And He does not need to change, for He is eternally perfect!

So every born-again believer has the perfect life of Christ within him or her. This is not the life of the human Jesus, but of the crucified, risen, ascended, glorified, victorious Christ. This is why it is made clear in John's gospel that the Holy Spirit would not be given until Christ was glorified! The Spirit led Jesus through the cross and resurrection enabling Him to overcome sin, the devil and death itself. **Now He lives in us to enable us to overcome! Or rather, He will overcome in and through us if we trust Him to do so!**

This is indeed good news. But it means we have to stop every self-improvement process we may have, and trust exclusively in Him instead.

So this is God's wisdom. His people could not obey Him or fulfil His will, no matter how determined they were. So He would do whatever was necessary to forgive their sins and failure, draw them back into relationship with Him and then come to live in them personally. Christ in them would obey the Father. All they would have to do was to trust Him to do this.

It would not even be a matter of the believer saying: "Help me to obey, Lord." But rather he would have to conclude: "Lord, there is nothing I can do in my own strength to obey you or please you. But I call on the Christ in me to work, so that He will do in me what truly pleases you. I submit myself to Him."

Because we are so used to trusting ourselves rather than Christ in us, we will need to understand some basic truths as to how this can be possible.

He is our righteousness

In His wisdom God has made Christ our righteousness.

We have seen that He took all our unrighteousness upon Himself when He went to the cross; all our sin, our failures, our unbelief and our fear. Through His sacrifice He has established a new righteousness that is given to those who put their faith in Him.

This gift of righteousness is Christ Himself. God does not give us a righteousness of our own. No, He makes Christ our righteousness, once we have been forgiven and cleansed of all unrighteousness. **If Christ is your righteousness, then God the Father accepts you as He accepts Christ!**

> *'This does not mean that we never sin. If we claim such a thing we only deceive ourselves and the truth does not live in us. Yet if we are honest with Him about our sins, He then forgives our sins and purifies us from everything that is not right in His eyes. He is always Faithful and Just in doing this.' (1 John 1:8-9)*

Why should I need a righteousness of my own, if God has given me Christ to be my righteousness? And this is His gift to every born-again believer!

It is impossible to improve on Christ as my righteousness. Any attempt of my own at being righteous would pale into insignificance compared with His righteousness.

To be righteous is to be 'justified' before God. This means that He declares me 'not guilty' and totally acceptable to Him. I have sinned, but Christ has never sinned. I am guilty but He is not guilty. So if God gives Him to be my righteousness He declares me to be not guilty!

Does this mean that it is of no consequence if I sin? By no means! In fact if I realise I have the sinless, righteous Christ living in me, this will turn me away from sin and will encourage me to resist temptation by trusting in the One who lives in Me! In my weakness as a human being I am prone to temptation. But the Christ in me has already overcome all temptation. So if I move aside and trust Him, the temptation will come to nothing, for it will not overcome the Christ within me! Christ in me will overcome the temptation.

I only have to be humble enough to admit that I cannot fight temptation in my own strength. **If I trust in Christ in me to overcome the temptation, He will never fail!**

So I need to build a relationship with the Christ within me. I can say: 'Over to you Lord. I cannot do this, but you can!'

Now this principle applies to just about any situation, not only temptation. I therefore live by this principle:

I cannot, but He can

If I do not, He will

But if I do, He will not!

Jesus said that in my flesh, my self-life, there dwells nothing good (John 6:63). If I believe that, I will not try to do things in my own strength. I will not want to promote myself, but the Christ who lives in me!

Jesus also said: *'But outside of Me you can do absolutely nothing'.* (John 15:5) If I believe that, I will not try to do anything apart from Him, for in His eyes anything done apart from Him is worthless; it will come to nothing and will produce no lasting fruit. And His purpose is that we should bear lasting fruit for the Father's glory:

> *'My Father will be glorified and honoured in your lives because you will bear much fruit and so demonstrate that you are truly My disciples.' (John 15:8)*

> *'You did not choose Me. No, it was I who chose you. But I do not only choose you to belong to Me; I also commission you to go and bear fruit that will be of eternal significance. As you go to do that, the Father will give you whatever you ask in My Name, those things that you know to be consistent with My will.' (John 15:16)*

So the rewards for bearing such fruit are great: we shall receive whatever we ask God to give us in the Name of Jesus!

I cannot do anything of eternal value with my self-life. **But nothing is impossible for the Christ within me.** If I choose not to try to accomplish things in my own power, but trust Him instead, then all things will become possible for me. **As Jesus said:** *'When you believe everything becomes possible.'* (Mark 9:23)

So the life of faith involves NOT trusting in myself but only in Christ within me. It is not even a partnership. I am not saying, 'Help me, Lord, to do this and that.' I am saying, 'I cannot do it, but you are able to do it in and through me.'

Now this seems straightforward enough when we are faced with things we know we cannot do ourselves, things we recognise to be totally beyond us. But what about things we can readily do in our own strength? Does the same principle apply then? Why not?

Are we to do things in our own strength and only call on the Christ within us when we are out of our depth, or faced with the seemingly impossible? At other times are we to say to the Lord: "You take a rest, Lord; I can handle this myself?" **Would it not be sensible to trust Him at all times?** Would not the results be much better if we used His supernatural power instead of only trusting in our natural abilities? Jesus was asked what we must do to accomplish the works God requires. He answered:

> *"'This is God's work," Jesus replied, "to believe in Me, the One He has sent."' (John 6:29)*

This is the work God requires of us, to trust in Jesus Christ, God's Son, the One He sent, who now lives in us in the person and power of His Spirit!

So what does it mean to walk in righteousness, to do what is right in God's sight? To trust in Christ within you. He will always do what is right and in the best possible way! Of course, He is expressing His life in and through us; so the results will not always be perfect because of the human factor. But they will be far better than if we trusted in ourselves!

He is our holiness

This is the next statement that Paul makes. He is our holiness as well as our righteousness.

God is holy. This is His nature. It is difficult to describe accurately what this means because He is so much greater than we are. But we can at least understand this: to say God is holy is to say that He is whole, complete, perfect in Himself! Whoever is holy is as He is. God's holy people are to reflect His character, who He is!

Remember that Jesus said that in our flesh life, our self-life, there is nothing good. So your flesh cannot reflect the person or the character of God, no matter how hard you try.

However, there is no point in trying to change yourself. Christ lives in you and He is your holiness. Whenever you allow Christ in you to express His life through you something of His person and character is revealed in positive ways.

You cannot change your flesh life. Not even God will try to do that, which is why you were crucified with Christ. God, in effect, said: "There is nothing to be done with that flesh life except for it to die."

Instead, He made your spirit alive by pouring His Spirit into you. Now Christ lives in you to express His life through you. **He does not try to change you, but He has exchanged your old life for a completely new life, Christ in you.**

Peter recalls God's command: *'Be holy, because I am holy'* (1 Peter 1:16). The only way that this command can be fulfilled is by allowing the holy life of Christ to be expressed through us.

Perhaps, like me, you cannot see how you could possibly live a holy life! I used to think like that until God showed me that the only way is to admit I cannot be holy in myself, but the One who lives in me is holy. If I defer to Him, His holiness will be expressed in what I say and do. This revelation changed my life. Instead of thinking it was impossible to obey such a command to be holy, I realised that God had made provision for me by putting the Holy One within me!

John also said that whoever claims to live in Him must demonstrate this by walking as Jesus did. (1 John 2:6) How can I possibly do that unless I trust in the Christ who lives within me? Only He could enable such a walk. And the scripture says this is not an option; it is a 'must'. **We *must* walk as Jesus** did! So there is no alternative; we have to trust in the Christ within us, and not in ourselves.

There is no point in excusing ourselves by saying that it does not appear that other Christians live like that. God will call us to account for how we live by His Word, not how well we have done in comparison with others!

So the only way I can fulfil God's purpose for me as a believer is not to trust in myself, but to trust in Christ in me.

Unfortunately the flesh itself is not dead, but we have died to the flesh. Even though Christ is alive in me, I can still desire what is unholy, have unholy thoughts, say and do unholy things. But if I defer to Christ He will enable me to think, speak and do that which is holy and pleasing to God.

So every day is full of choices. Do I give way to my own desires, or deny myself in order to please the Lord, trusting in Christ instead? Jesus told His disciples:

> *'If anyone makes the decision to be My follower, he will have to deny what he wants for himself. He must be prepared to suffer willingly any cross of sacrifice asked of him; then he can follow Me.' (Matt. 16:24)*

There is no option for the faithful believer. To follow Jesus, to work as He did, must involve a denying of that self-life, with its unholy desires. Jesus went on to explain:

> *'For whoever is intent only on his own welfare will lose his life eternally. But whoever is prepared to lose his life for Me will find eternal life.' (Matt. 16:25)*

Naturally, we want to do everything we can to keep hold of that self-life. We are afraid that somehow we will lose our identity, or we will lose control of our lives. In one sense this is exactly what we need to do: **to lose the old identity of being without Christ in us, and discover our new identity: Christ in us, the hope of glory!**

The more we trust in Him, the more we will discover this new identity. So I can choose to indulge myself and ignore the Lord, or deny myself and please the Lord. The choice is clear and is the same for every believer.

If I believe there is nothing good in that self-life then it will not be difficult to deny myself. But if I am proud I will not want to deny myself. If I value my own opinions rather than God's Word, if I want others to admire me, then I will want to promote myself, not deny myself. **But unless I deny myself I cannot follow Christ and He cannot express His life in and through me.**

> **I cannot, but He can**
> **If I do not, He will**
> **But if I do, He will not!**

It is not a matter of saying, "Lord, help me to express your life in who I am", or of praying, "Change me, Lord, so I am more like you." This is a common mistake that Christians make because they misunderstand what Paul says about being changed into His likeness from one degree of glory to another.

Paul does not intend us to imagine that this self life, in which there is nothing good, can be changed into the likeness of Christ. No, the more we deny ourselves and allow the Christ in us to express His life through us, the more we reflect the glory of the One who lives in us. **So it will appear to others that we are more Christ-like because more of Him is being expressed in our lives, and therefore less of self.**

We are not changed, but transformed, which is the meaning of the original, the same word used of Jesus when He was transfigured before the three disciples on the high mountain. **Something of God's glory is revealed through us every time we allow the Christ in us to be expressed in our lives.**

I have no righteousness of my own; but Christ is my righteousness. I have no holiness of my own; but Christ is my holiness.

If I do not try to do things in my own strength but trust Him, then He will always work in me and through me; and the results will be good. But if I insist on doing things myself, He will not prevent me from doing so. He will simply wait until I am ready to trust Him again.

Of course, the Lord wants to bring us to a place where we enjoy a continual dialogue with Him, what Paul calls 'praying continually.' The Lord never leaves us, but He does leave us to our own devices when we take the initiative away from Him. Better to defer to Him at all times. It is not difficult to do this; it is simply a matter of choice!

He is our redemption

To say that we are redeemed is to say that we have been purchased by the blood of Jesus so that our lives rightly belong to God.

> *'God has purchased you for Himself; He has paid the price*
> *for you with His Son's blood. So honour Him in the way*
> *you use your body!' (1 Cor. 6:20)*

He is the One who redeemed us through the sacrifice He made for us. And so He Himself is our redemption. We belong totally to the Lord; that is our security. It is important to be clear as to the ownership of your life. **We are His; we do not belong to ourselves. If you belong to Him, then He wants to express His life in and through you, His divine, righteous, holy, eternal life!**

I belong to God because I am in Christ and He lives in me. I could never be any closer to Him. He wants me to know and enjoy that intimate relationship with Him. This is the evidence of how He has already loved me, and has already loved you. He has already redeemed you, already paid the price for you. You already belong to Him; you are His child, His son, His daughter. And so He is your Father who has placed His Son in you that you might live in unity with your Father in heaven.

Jesus addressed Him in prayer as 'Holy Father', 'Righteous Father', 'Heavenly Father.' It is a wonderful truth that we are already one with the Father because we live in Christ and He in us. **We are no longer separated from Him by sin; we are one with Him.**

How often we need to be reminded of these truths so that we will truly believe them and live in the good of them. So the Father calls you His 'beloved one.' He is always ready to hear you and act in your life because His Son lives in you, and you are never separated from His love. Paul said that in every hardship or difficulty *'we are more than victorious through Him, for He has already won the victory for us and demonstrated such love for us'* (Rom. 8:37).

A conqueror is someone who fights a battle and wins. You are more than a conqueror if you are given the victory, for the One within you has fought the battle on your behalf. **The One who has already overcome all opposition on the cross now lives in you and if you trust in Him, He gives you the victory.** So Paul concludes:

'I am totally convinced that death cannot separate us from Him or His love. Neither can anything that could ever happen to us in this life! No angels can stand in the way of God's personal love for us, nor can any demons prevent that love. Nothing in the present, nor anything that could happen in the future, would be able to destroy God's love for us. There is no spiritual power, nor any created power, that will ever be able to separate us from God's love for us that has already been so clearly expressed in Christ Jesus our Lord.' (Rom. 8:38-39)

Jesus even said:

'If anyone genuinely loves Me, he will put My teaching into practice. My Father will love him and both He and I will come and live with him. Yes, we will make our home with him.' (John 14:23)

We can love Him because He has first loved us by dying for us, then giving Himself to live in us. **We have His love and power within us to enable us to obey Him.** He commands us to believe in Him and to love others as He has loved us. How could we possibly do that unless He has placed His own love in us?

We still have to make the decisions to believe and love. When we do so, then the Christ in us can work through us and reveal something of His glory and victory! John says:

'Those who obey His commands show they continue to live in Him, and He lives in them. We can be sure that He does live in us because He has given us His Spirit.' (1 John 3:24)

All of us have difficulties to face; life on earth is like that. How wonderful to know that we are able to overcome because the Victor lives in us and our trust is in Him. John said:

'Everyone who has received the new birth that God gives, overcomes the spirit that influences the world around him. It is our faith in Jesus and what He has done that has given us victory over worldliness. I ask you, "Who has really overcome this worldliness?" Obviously only he who believes and trusts in Jesus as God's victorious Son.' (1 John 5:4-5)

What truth! Everyone who is born-again has this victory within his or her reach. And look what this scripture reveals. **Your faith has *already* overcome worldliness! That is the power of the faith that God has given you!** For He is the Author of your faith.

All this is possible for you because Jesus Christ is your redemption as well as your righteousness and holiness. **He has truly done the complete work for you on the cross and now lives in you to see the outworking of His victory in your life.**

How tragic that so many Christians live with Christ in them and yet still trust in themselves, because they have never received revelation of the truth. How blessed you are that the Holy Spirit bears witness to the truth of God's Word, so that now you can live in the good of these wonderful truths!

He is your life

Your new life is Christ in you. He personally is your new life. John says:

'So he who belongs to Jesus has this life; but he who does not belong to Jesus does not have that life.' (1 John 5:12)

Jesus Christ is the person of God. The Holy Spirit is the person of God. So you have the person of Christ living in you. Therefore you have every aspect of His life that you will ever need already in you. You have His love, His mercy, His peace, His compassion, His power, His healing, and so on.

The problem for many Christians is that they keep asking God for what He has already given them. **We are to believe that He has already given what He has given, and then we can live in the good of what He has given.** Jesus said:

> *'So I tell you, no matter what you ask in prayer, believe it is*
> *yours already, and it will be yours!' (Mark 11:24)*

If you believe that Christ is in you, then the answer to your need is already within you. The prayer of faith releases within you whatever you need of Christ's life because the fullness of that life is already in you! That life is yours to lay hold of and see released through your life.

To ask for what you already have is to doubt that you have what God says you have, what He has given you already. So we need to ask Him to forgive such unbelief and lack of faith, thanking Him that we have the fullness of the life of Christ.

It is obvious that you can only express in your life what you believe you have! If you believe you have the life of Christ within you, then you can express His life in your life. To others it will seem that this is your life, but in reality it will be His life in you.

This was the revelation that took place in the lives of Jesus' original disciples in fulfilment of the series of promises He gave them at the Last Supper. The Spirit of Truth who had been with them in the person of Jesus would be in them after Jesus' return to heaven. Everything in Jesus' teaching and His relationship with the disciples was leading to the point when He said to them:

> *'Stay living in Me and I will continue to live in you. It is*
> *impossible for any branch to be fruitful if it is separated*
> *from the Vine. It has to continue to live in the Vine. In the*
> *same way it would be impossible for you to bear fruit if you*
> *were not to remain living in Me.' (John 15:4)*

This was a revolutionary statement which the disciples probably could not understand when they first heard it. Once they had received the Holy Spirit, then they could begin to appreciate what Jesus had meant. Now they had His life in them, not simply with them, His works could be expressed through them. In other words, Jesus would continue His ministry in the world in them, and in others who came to believe in Him. So He made this extraordinary promise:

'I tell you the truth, anyone who puts his faith in Me will do the same things that I have been doing. He will be able to do even greater things than these because of what will happen when I return to be with the Father.' (John 14:12)

Clearly believers can only do the same things as Jesus if they possess His own life and power. There is no way that we can imitate His life and actions through our own human strength. To suggest to people that this is what they ought to do, will only produce in them an inevitable sense of failure and even condemnation.

But once a believer learns to trust in Christ in him or her, then it becomes obvious that He can express His life through that believer and can perform mighty things through him or her.

Why should Jesus clearly state that believers will do even greater things than He did during His humanity on earth? During that time He was limited by the restrictions of His humanity. **But the risen Christ who lives in us has overcome sin, the devil and death. Now He reigns in heavenly glory without any limitations or restrictions.**

Now believers can do what Jesus could not do during His humanity. They can pray for Him to come and live in people in the person and power of His Spirit. Such blessing was only possible once He had returned to the Father, as He made clear in what He said at the Last Supper.

So the risen, glorified, triumphant Christ is now your life, the new life within you. This is your new identity: Christ in you.

Potentially there are no limits to what He can do through you, if you allow Him to express His life in you.

So your key truth is: 'Not I, but Christ in me.' There are many things I cannot do myself, but all things are possible for Him. If I stop trying to do things in my own strength, He will do them in and through me by His power. But if I persist in doing things myself, He will wait until I again trust in Him.

CHAPTER 4

MY WEAKNESS DOES
NOT MATTER

Paul was an extremely clever and able person. Although only a young man when he met with Jesus on the road to Damascus, he was already a rising star in his religion, Judaism. Some years later, after receiving personally great revelations from Jesus Christ, he was taught a very important lesson by his Lord.

'Although there is nothing to be gained from it, I will show you that I have good cause to boast. I will tell of visions and revelations I have received from the Lord.

Fourteen years ago I was caught up in a vision to the third heaven, into paradise itself. I could not tell whether my spirit was still in my body or had momentarily left it. I really do not know, but God knows. But I am sure that I was lifted up into paradise and heard things I cannot express, that should not be told to anyone.'

A person who has had such an experience has something to boast about. But I do not claim any credit for this myself. I will only boast about my personal weaknesses. I could not be accused of speaking foolishly if I did boast about such experiences, for I only speak the truth about what happened. But I will not go into detail, for I do not want to promote myself. I want people to judge me by what I say and do, not by the revelations I have received.

And the Lord ensured I would not be puffed up with pride, for I was given a thorn in my flesh to stop me from being

proud because of these great encounters. This thorn was a
messenger from Satan, someone he sent to torment me.

I pleaded with the Lord on three occasions for this 'thorn' to
be taken away. 'My grace is always sufficient to meet your
need,' He told me; 'My power is revealed more perfectly
through your weakness!' This is why I am happy to boast
about my weaknesses, for then Christ's power will work
through me.' (2 Cor. 12:1-9)

The Lord first says to Paul: 'My grace is sufficient for you.' What is this
grace? Paul has already spoken of this earlier in the same letter:

'You are well aware of the nature of the grace our Lord Jesus
Christ has demonstrated. In heaven He was rich beyond
measure, yet for your sakes He came to share the poverty
of our humanity, so that now through that poverty you are
able to share in His heavenly riches.' (2 Cor. 8:9)

We can now see what this means. Jesus, who reigned in glory and majesty
in heaven, became poor in the sense that he came to share in the poverty and
restrictions of our humanity. He came not to be served, but to serve and to
give His life as a ransom for many!

So He was sent to earth by the Father for us. Now, because of all He did
for us on earth, we are able to share in His risen, glorified life. **The glorified
Christ lives within us making us truly rich, not only in this life but for all
eternity!**

With Christ living in you, there is no doubt that you are truly rich. His
life has become your life! This is His gracious gift to you. You deserved nothing from God except to be judged, condemned and punished for your sins and
disobedience. Instead He has forgiven you and has given you the very best He
has to give – His own Son! You are truly rich! Paul says:

'I am always thankful to God for you because He has shown
you so much grace through your union with Christ Jesus.
Because you live in Christ, you have been blessed with all

His riches. He has blessed you in every conceivable way. You know that all His riches are yours and you are able to speak His many blessings over your lives. This is possible because all we taught you about Christ was imparted to you when you believed in Him. For this reason you do not lack any of His spiritual gifts. They are yours to enable you to persevere in faith as you look with eager expectation for our Lord Jesus Christ to be revealed in His full majesty and glory.' (1 Cor. 1:4-7)

God has certainly been gracious to you! **Because you have been made one with Christ you have already been enriched in every way.** You can know His riches and speak His blessings over your life. He will speak through you and will give you all the revelation knowledge that you need.

With Christ in you, every spiritual gift has been given to you and is available for you to use whenever appropriate. Now He wants His grace to be extended to others through you.

He wants you to be merciful for He is merciful. Jesus made it clear that whenever a believer prays, it is imperative for him or her to forgive anyone who has sinned against or offended him or her. Failure to forgive others will result in God refusing to forgive the believer.

God has been so merciful and gracious to us, it is essential for us to be merciful and gracious to others. Jesus said He had not come to judge but to serve. So we are not to judge, or we will be judged with the same judgment with which we judge others.

The Christ in you is merciful, full of grace and chooses not to judge, even though all judgment has been entrusted to Him by the Father.

There will probably be many situations when you in your natural self will not want to be merciful and forgive. You may even feel justified in judging others, especially if they are obviously guilty of sin. There will be times when you will not feel like being gracious. You will not want to give to others or to bless them. You may be full of self-pity instead of being ready to be compassionate towards others.

However, the Christ in you is always ready to be merciful and to forgive; He is always ready to bless and to give. He never wants to judge through you. So in all these ways we recognise our own weakness; but the life of Christ within us never changes. So His grace is always sufficient for us, irrespective of the circumstances.

This was the lesson God was teaching Paul. His grace was sufficient to enable him to cope with any or every situation. However, he goes further still:

> *'My power is revealed more perfectly through your weakness' (2 Cor. 12:9)*

If we recognise that in fulfilling God's will we are weak and ineffective in ourselves, then we can trust in the power of Christ to work in and through us. So it is a good and positive thing to recognise your own weakness.

Many Christians make the mistake of asking God to make them stronger. That seems to be a good, worthwhile prayer, but in fact it is the very opposite! I believe God's attitude is to say in effect: 'You do enough damage in your weakness. If I was to make you stronger, you would do even more damage!'

He wants us to remain weak in ourselves. Paul even says that we are weak in Christ. But He is the strength of our life. So if we trust in Him instead of ourselves His strength and His power will be released in and through us. We can do all things through Him who gives us strength. We certainly cannot do all things in our own strength, but we can by trusting in His power. Paul says that God is able to do so much more than all you would ever dare to ask Him or even imagine that He would give you through His power that He has already placed within you. (Eph. 3:20)

In ourselves we are to remain weak. In Him and with His presence in us, the strength and power of His life can be expressed in us. So Paul goes on to say:

> *'"My grace is always sufficient to meet your need," He told me; "My power is revealed more perfectly through your weakness!" This is why I am happy to boast about My weaknesses, for then Christ's power will work through me.' (2 Cor. 12:9)*

Paul is prepared to parade his weaknesses openly. This flies in the face of certain so-called faith teachers who say that you should never speak of any weakness in your life! Paul understands the truth far better. The more open he is about his weakness, the more he will depend on God's power. In fact he says that this power rests or remains on him because he is open about his own weakness!

What does this have to say to us? That our weakness really does not matter, so long as we trust in the power of Christ within us! This is good news, for the world is full of Christians who are striving to be stronger, and who feel they are failures because they are weak. They are even made to feel bad about being weak by those who want to appear strong!

Remember that God allowed Paul to have this thorn in his flesh to teach him this valuable spiritual lesson. In this statement Paul shows true spirituality. Not only does he openly admit his weaknesses, he rejoices or delights in them. And he does this 'for Christ's sake'! This is His purpose. So you can rejoice that you are weak in yourself and do not have to try to make yourself stronger. For Christ in you is the strength of your life and when you boast about your weakness, the power of Christ rests upon you.

Of course it is unbelief to speak negatively of yourself without immediately confessing the truth about Christ in you! So you do not think or speak about yourself as a no-good, useless failure. Because you place your life under the words you speak, you need to speak the truth of who you are in Christ, with Christ living in you. Then you will be positive, not negative in your attitudes.

Many of Paul's experiences kept him aware of his personal weakness, but also dependent on the Christ who was not only with him, but within him! He could rejoice in the way he was persecuted, for this is obedience to what Jesus commanded His disciples to do in the face of persecution.

Paul could rejoice in all his hardship and difficulties because every one of these experiences told him to remain dependent on Christ, and so enable Christ to give him the victory over his circumstances. And what a testing he had:

> *'No, we are able to commend ourselves in every way because*
> *of the cost we have been prepared to embrace for the cause*
> *of the gospel. We have needed great endurance in the face*
> *of many difficulties and hardships, and in circumstances*

that have caused much distress. We have suffered floggings, imprisonment and even riots. We certainly have worked hard and have known what it is to be without sleep and food. We have had to live in purity. We have needed understanding, patience and kindness. We have followed the leading of the Holy Spirit and have acted with love. We have spoken the truth and have been instruments of God's power. We have needed to use the spiritual weapons of righteousness to be on the offensive and also in self-defence. We have known times of glory and yet have been treated with dishonour. Sometimes we have been praised, at other times we have been slandered. Although we are genuine we have been regarded by some as impostors. Sometimes we are well known, in other places nobody knows who we are. We have been close to death, but we are still here! We have been beaten, but not killed. Even in times of sorrow we have continued to rejoice. Even when poor ourselves, we have been able to make many rich through what they have received from God. We have nothing ourselves, yet truly we have everything in Christ!' (2 Cor. 6:4-10)

Such experiences taught Paul to depend entirely on God and not himself. Christ in him sustained him throughout his ministry. And tremendous fruit resulted from his life of persevering faith. So Paul's conclusion was simple:

'Yes, for Christ's sake, I even delight in being so weak, in suffering rejection and hardships, in being persecuted and having to face so many difficulties. For the more I am aware of my own weakness, the more I can depend on His strength.' (2 Cor. 12:10)

And this is true for you also. **You are weak in yourself, but strong in Christ Jesus, with Christ in you!**

What a blessing to realise that our weakness does not matter, that it is an asset even, so long as in our weakness we place our trust in the One who is our strength!

In my ministry I have experienced opposition, persecution, and people spreading untrue things about me. I learned to be like Jesus when He was accused falsely. He said nothing. The Lord would encourage me at such times by saying: "Colin, you know the truth and I know the truth, and that is all that matters." Then, like Paul, I would rejoice and give thanks that such experiences encouraged me to remember that I am nothing, but my identity is in Christ and He in me. And nobody, nor any experience, can ever separate me from Him. The greater the opposition, the greater my dependence on Him.

Humanly speaking, it is never easy to have to work through such experiences. But Jesus makes it clear that anyone coming against you is actually coming against Him. So it is not for you to retaliate, but to leave the issue in His hands. The Christ in you is now your shield and defence. **Opposition helps to keep you humble and dependent on Christ in you!**

You can be thankful that your focus can be, not on your own weakness, but on the power of Christ who lives in you!

CHAPTER 5

NOT I BUT CHRIST

In every situation this is the principle by which you can live: Not I, but Christ who lives in me! Now we must see how to apply this principle in practice, and what difficulties we may face in seeking to do so.

These are the alternatives: either I am going to speak, or Christ will speak through me. Either I am going to act or Christ will act through me.

What we say

We must first understand that whenever Christ speaks through us, we still have to speak! The difference is the source from which the words come. If I am to speak then I have to decide what I am going to say, using my own intelligence and reasoning abilities. What I say could be in line with God's Word, or I could be expressing some opinions of my own that contradict His Word. On a number of occasions Peter is remembered for making the mistake of speaking with his own understanding, even if this contradicted what Jesus said. For example, one moment Peter was the mouthpiece of God the Father in proclaiming Jesus to be God's Son, the Messiah. Now they knew who He was, Jesus used this opportunity to tell the disciples that He would be rejected, ill-treated, crucified, but that He would be raised from the dead on the third day.

Peter took Jesus aside and contradicted what He had just said, becoming, at that moment, the mouthpiece of the devil who stands against the truth. Why did Peter make such an error? Because he trusted in his own understanding of what would happen to the Messiah, who was expected to triumph over His enemies, not be put to death by them!

James warns us that the wrong use of the mouth can be dangerous. He likens the tongue to the rudder of a ship. It is a very small part, but directs the course in which the whole vessel is steered.

So what we say directs the course of our lives. This is because we can have many conflicting thoughts going on within our minds, but when we speak we have decided which of these thoughts we believe. James warns:

> *'In the same way the tongue is only a tiny part of your body, but it can do great harm. A forest fire can be started by a small spark!' (James 3:5)*

What you say can either glorify God, or can do great damage to yourself or to others!

> *'We use the tongue to praise our Lord and Father and yet we can also use it to speak curse over people, who God has made in His image. So out of the same mouth comes both praise and curse. My brothers, obviously this should not be the case. How can fresh water and salt water flow out of the same spring? My friends, is it possible for a fig tree to produce olives, or for a vine to produce figs? Well, it is impossible for a salt spring to produce fresh water.' (James 3:9-12)*

Obviously it is the source from which we speak that determines the power of what we say, for good or ill. Jesus warned that, *'a person speaks from the overflow of his heart'*. (Matt. 12:34) So the condition of the heart will determine the relative value of what we say. Jesus also warned:

> *'So I tell you clearly that every man will have to give account on Judgment Day for every careless word he has spoken. For by your words you will be declared innocent and by the words you have spoken you will be condemned.' (Matt. 12:36-37)*

These are surely some of the most awesome words that Jesus spoke. They demonstrate how important it is to set our hearts on the truth so that we speak the truth. And truth is a person! Jesus said: "I AM THE TRUTH." (John 14:6)

The Truth lives in you! You have been given the Spirit of Truth who is to guide you into all truth. Jesus said:

> *'But when the Spirit of Truth comes He will give you the complete revelation of the Truth.' (John 16:13-14)*

> *'The Father will send you the Counsellor, the Holy Spirit, in My Name. When He comes He will teach you all you need to know and will remind you of everything I have already taught you.' (John 14:26)*

So the Holy Spirit points us to Jesus, to what He has said and done. He wants to keep our focus on the truth so that we will speak according to the truth, and not according to our own ideas or opinions.

Here the scriptures are a great help to us, for this is the revelation of the truth that God has handed down to us. We can check what we think, what we believe and therefore speak, with what is written in God's Word. Only then are we sure whether what we have said is the truth, or is some form of deception or error.

How important, then, for us to be men and women of the Word. The more we know the revelation of the truth in the New Testament, the more certain we can be that what we say is in line with what Jesus has said.

One of the most common sins in the world today is committed when people exalt their reason above the revelation of truth that God has given us. This is great pride for it is saying: "I know better than God!" or "Never mind what God says, this is what I think!" People may even suggest that God's Word is out of date. This is certainly not true, for Jesus has the words of eternal life and He says:

> *'The heavens and the earth will end, but My words are eternal and will remain forever.' (Matt. 24:35)*

God's truth can never be out of date. Truth is eternal. His Word is the same for every successive generation! It is simply a matter of whether we believe the revelation of truth or not! If our hearts are set on the truth, we will speak the truth with the love of Christ within us.

Governments may legislate for what they permit lawfully in modern society. But God's view of what is righteous or sinful never changes. No government will ever change God's mind, neither can they alter the Truth, the person of Jesus Christ.

So we Christians need to set the example of speaking the truth from our hearts, ensuring that all we say is in line with God's Word and does not contradict what He says. This involves not only becoming men and women who read, listen to and study God's Word, but that we are those who submit our minds, our thinking to the revelation of the Truth.

I have often heard it suggested that this is to limit our powers of thinking and reasoning that have been given to us by God. But this is far from the case. The natural mind can only think naturally; God's Word is supernatural, as is His Holy Spirit who lives in us. To have your mind informed by God's Word and the Holy Spirit will therefore expand your thinking to include the supernatural.

When Jesus told the disciples to feed the multitudes, they responded with their reason. 'Where can we buy bread in this remote place?' 'It would cost nearly a year's wages to give each one just a little.' This sounds very reasonable and sensible; but the scripture says that Jesus already knew what He would do. Why? Because He looked at the situation from a supernatural perspective. So even though He only had a little boy's picnic to work with, the whole multitude was fed and the disciples collected twelve basketfuls of the remains.

Jesus thought expansively. He does not limit us to our natural powers of reason; He takes us beyond reason into the realms of faith. The risen, victorious Christ lives in you. So as you submit your natural mind to the mind of Christ you will think, believe, speak and act expansively, with supernatural wisdom and power. **He does not want to limit your thinking, but to expand it to include all that is possible through His supernatural power.**

The scripture is clear, because Christ is in you, you now have the mind of Christ! But you also have your natural mind. It is a question of which you choose to employ, your natural mind or the mind of Christ. Which is going to dominate and be placed in control in your life? Is Christ going to be placed on the throne of your life, or are you going to put self, with your own limited reasoning powers, on the throne?

It is not a matter of exalting His Word above your own thoughts, ideas and opinions only occasionally, when it suits you or when you feel it is necessary to do so. Jesus Christ needs to remain permanently on the throne of your life. As Jesus warned His disciples, this will involve denying yourself daily, denying any thoughts that conflict with the truth. It involves realising that your opinions are worthless in God's eyes. The Holy Spirit lives in you to guide you into all the truth, not your opinions!

The power of our words is extensive, directing the course of our lives. We want to speak the truth so that we walk in the truth. John wrote:

> *'It gave me great joy when some brothers came and testified*
> *that you live in the truth, and told of how you continue to*
> *walk in the truth. There can be no greater joy for me than*
> *to hear of my spiritual children walking in the truth.' (3*
> *John v. 3)*

This is the principle John learned from Jesus Himself. But we will only walk in the truth if we speak the truth; and we will only speak the truth if we know the truth and have submitted ourselves to Jesus Christ who lives in us. For then we will not want to rise up in rebellion against what He says.

We also need to understand the power of the truth and therefore the power in the words of Jesus Christ. He said: '*The words I have spoken to you contain the life of God's Spirit.*' (John 6:63)

God's life is in His words. How did He create? He spoke and Jesus Christ, the Word of God, went forth and brought all creation into being. How did Jesus heal? He spoke. 'Get up and walk,' and the crippled were healed. 'Be opened' and blind eyes, deaf ears and dumb mouths were opened. 'Your faith has healed you' and miracles took place. 'Go' and two thousand demons left a demented man and went into a herd of pigs.

That same Jesus Christ now lives in you. If He speaks through you such things can happen today! In your experience! Do not limit Him by your reason or unbelief. Remember that at Nazareth even Jesus could not perform many miracles because of the unbelief of the people!

See what is potentially possible, not for you in your natural weakness, but for the Christ who lives in you and who is able to work through you despite your weakness.

You speak in His Name when Christ is allowed to speak through you. This does not mean that you merely use the Name of Jesus Christ, powerful though His Name is; but it means you speak and act on His behalf, or, in other words, He speaks and acts through you. Paul writes:

> *'Be sure that no matter what you say or do, you are able to do everything in the name of Jesus, because you do what pleases Him, and you do it with thankfulness to God the Father because of all you receive in His Son.' (Col. 3:17)*

The apostle is not speaking of an occasional utterance or action; he speaks about whatever you do or say! In other words, God wants to teach us to allow the Christ in us to be expressed through us continually! This is going to require a radical change of approach for most people, who have spent their lives depending on themselves, their own natural understanding and resources. However such a change is essential if you are to allow the Christ in you to work through you in the ways He intends.

Whenever I preach, teach or write I trust Christ to speak through me, to give me the right words. I have done this for over 40 years and have learned so much myself in the process. I listen as I speak and learn from what I say because the source of the words is not my limited understanding, but the Spirit of the risen Christ who lives in me.

I have nothing I want to say; He gives me the words to say. So I am receiving revelation, along with everyone else who is listening.

Do I prepare to speak? Most certainly, even though I do not have a prepared text from which to speak. I have to be in the place of unity and submission to the Lord, confident that He will speak through me. There may be thousands of people present or just a handful, but the principle is the same; I want Christ to speak through me. Not I, but Christ!

I remember one occasion when I was praying before a meeting and God told me to preach on a particular passage of scripture. I said to Him: "But, Lord, I don't understand what those verses mean." To which He replied: "Well, you will once you have preached on them!"

And that turned out to be the case. By the end of the sermon I understood because of the revelation the Spirit of Christ had brought through what I said.

This is an exciting way to preach! But it is not a recipe for those learning to be preachers. I tell our Bible College students not to try to preach in that way until they are in the place of submission to Christ so that they know He will speak through them.

This principle was dramatically demonstrated one day when I was recording a series of programmes for my daily radio broadcast that is transmitted several times a day. I was feeling very tired because I had been so busy. During one of the programmes I fell asleep while speaking! Yet I continued to speak! Some minutes later I awoke and was still speaking but without any idea of what I had said while asleep.

At the time this was an unnerving experience, for the words were continuing to flow out of my mouth. So I thought, 'I had better let the words continue to flow and not interrupt!'

When I finished speaking I said to Julia Fisher, who was in the studio with me as she presents the programmes, "Julia, did what I said make sense?" "Yes", she replied, "it made perfect sense. It was clearly anointed. But why do you ask?" I answered: "Because I fell asleep in the middle of the message and I haven't a clue as to what I said."

Afterwards I realised how this is a classic example of, 'Not I, but Christ!' I have heard of congregations falling asleep during the preaching, but never the preacher himself falling asleep!

By the way, I was really asleep. You know how you feel refreshed after a cat-nap. Well after this incident I was refreshed and completed the recording session with renewed energy. 'Not I, but Christ!'

On many occasions when dealing with people's personal problems, I have not known what to say in reference to some of the exceedingly difficult situations I have heard described. So I pray quietly: "Lord, I don't know what to say: please speak through me." In His love for the person before me He does, because He wants to meet that person's need. He wants to speak from His heart into the heart of that person. I am only the mouthpiece.

He will readily speak through you if you trust Him to do so! He will give you words of wisdom that will often unlock the situations that seem so desperate. I learned that it was futile for me to try to answer such needs with my own wisdom and understanding, even after so many years of experience in ministry. **It is a question of being humble enough to say, "Over to you, Lord." He will always make a better job of dealing with the situation!**

When I was a young pastor God taught me an important lesson about this subject. A woman who I did not know came to speak to me about a pastoral problem. As I was listening to her, I knew the answer to her dilemma. So when she had finished speaking I explained to her what she needed to do. She looked at me obviously perplexed!

So I went over the solution again and again. Still she did not understand, although the answer was so clear to me. I finally suggested that we prayed together. When we did so, God gave me a word for her, just a single sentence. The woman jumped to her feet while I was still praying and said: "That's it! That is what I needed to hear. Thank you very much." And she walked out of my office.

I heard later that this simple sentence from God had completely resolved the situation. The strange thing is this. What the Lord said was in agreement with what I had been telling the lady, but He said it in a way she could understand and receive it. That is the wisdom of the Spirit of Christ within!

From that incident I learned to go into prayer as soon as possible, and to expect Christ to speak through me in precisely the right way, from His heart to the heart of the person concerned!

I teach our Bible College students to listen with one ear to what the person is saying, and with the other ear to what the Spirit is saying about the situation. He will always speak the truth and show you what you cannot understand with your natural mind. Remember, you have the mind of Christ; so use it! Draw on His wisdom by the Holy Spirit.

Often we learn from our mistakes. It has been said that there are no mistakes in the Lord, except those from which you do not learn! I share these incidents with you because I want you to appreciate that it is a process of learning to trust Christ instead of ourselves, learning to defer to Him. So do not be discouraged if, at first, you seem to fail to do this on several occasions. And do not allow the enemy to place you under any false condemnation for such failures. The Holy Spirit is a good teacher and He will not give up on you. He lives in you and will not leave you because you have ignored Him or misunderstood something He said. He will not reject you if you disobey something He tells you to do. He will wait for you to ask for God's forgiveness, and will then continue to speak to you and work in and through you for the Father's glory!

Whatever we do

Often actions need to accompany the words we speak. The Spirit of Christ will not only speak through us; He will work through us! Jesus says that the Father will be glorified by the fruit that we bear. In reality this fruit is produced by the work of the Spirit within us.

If Christ is in us, then we can do the same works as He did. But this is true not only of healings, miracles, signs and wonders, but also of the multitude of minor, seemingly less impressive, things that we can do whenever we deny ourselves and allow the Christ in us to manifest His life through us. David uses a very useful illustration when speaking of himself:

> *'But I am like an olive tree flourishing in the house of God;*
> *I trust in God's unfailing love for ever and ever. I will*
> *praise you forever for what you have done; in your name*
> *I will hope, for your name is good. I will praise you in the*
> *presence of your saints.' (Psalm 52:8-9 NIV)*

Imagine an olive tree at harvest time. It is covered by thousands of tiny olives, the fruit the tree has produced. Then see yourself as the olive tree. Each olive is small but it represents an occasion when you denied yourself and allowed the life and love of Christ to be expressed through you. These are not necessarily the great mighty miracles of power. They are the acts of selfless love, of kindness and goodness that flow from your life through the Spirit of Christ. They represent every occasion when you denied doing what you wanted to do and did what God wanted you to do instead. These 'olives' contain oil, which in scripture signifies the Holy Spirit!

Every olive represents an occasion when you stood aside and allowed the Christ in you to operate instead. These olives are produced whenever you said, "Lord I cannot but you can. So I will not and you will act through me." Small acts of love, of giving graciously to others. Every act of mercy and forgiveness. Every act of obedience to the leading of the Holy Spirit. Every occasion when you acted on God's Word. Every time that you have been faithful to the Lord in being what He wants you to be, and doing what He wants you to do.

Every day you can produce many olives on your tree! They are in truth the results of the Spirit of Christ working in and through you, so all the glory goes to Him. It is not a matter of saying, 'Look how much fruit I have produced,' but rather of saying like David: *'I will praise you forever for what you have done.'* (Psalm 52:9)

Of course there will also be the occasions when you produce an 'apple' or an 'orange', a work of greater power, or a supernatural miracle. There may even be some 'grapefruits' or 'melons', amazing things that you could never have imagined God would do through you! But do not see these as the only fruit you are to produce.

Every time you impact the life of someone else with the life or the love of Christ you are being fruitful. Every time you do through Him what you could never do through your natural life, you are bearing fruit! Whenever you lead someone to faith in Christ Jesus, when you pray for others, when you love and care for those that naturally you would not want to love or feel able to love, you are being fruitful. The possibilities are limitless!

God has prepared good works for each one of us to accomplish in His Name, on His behalf. There are works He knows we will do because we trust in Him. These are the works of faith. James wrote:

> *'My brothers, of what value is the faith a man claims to have if that faith is not reflected in his actions? Does he really possess the faith that can save him?*
>
> *For example, suppose a brother or sister needs clothing and food. If anyone of you was to say, 'God bless you; keep warm and well fed,' but did nothing to relieve his physical needs, what good would your faith be? So you can see that unless faith gives birth to action, it is dead!*
>
> *Someone may say, 'You have faith; I do practical things.' Well, show your faith without positive actions, and I will show you that my faith is genuine because of what I do!'* (James 2:14-18)

True faith produces the works of faith. It is not a matter of producing works in an attempt to receive salvation; these are the deeds we perform because we have already received salvation, because Christ is working in and through us! Jesus spoke of the separation between the sheep and the goats:

'When the Son of Man returns He will come in glory attended by angels; and He will sit on His throne in heavenly glory. All the nations will be gathered before Him and as a shepherd separates the sheep from the goats, so He will divide the people into two groups. Those who are His sheep He will place on His right; the goats will be on His left.'
(Matt. 25:31-33)

He goes on to say that the sheep are those who did what God wanted of them. They gave themselves to others in various ways. In other words, they allowed the Christ within them to express His love through Him. **God's love expressed in our lives always results in positive action:**

'The King will say to the sheep on His right, "You are blessed by My Father. So come and claim your inheritance, the Kingdom He prepared for you since creation began. For you fed Me when I was hungry and you satisfied My thirst. When I came to you in the form of a stranger, you invited Me in to stay. When I needed clothing you gave Me clothes. When I was sick you cared for Me. And when I was in prison you came and visited Me."' *(Matt. 25:34-36)*

The sheep are amazed at the Lord's commendation, for they have done what clearly seemed right and natural for them, because of their desire to please the Lord and allow His life to be expressed through their lives:

'Then the righteous, the sheep, will answer, "Lord, when did we see You hungry and feed You or when did we satisfy Your thirst? When did we invite You in as a stranger or clothe You? When did we see You sick or in prison and visit You?"

The King will then reply, "I tell you the truth, whatever you did for another person, who I regard as My brother, you actually did for Me."' *(Matt. 25:37-40)*

Notice the content of the commendation. Jesus identifies personally with all those people in need and calls them His brothers, because He came to share in their humanity. The goats do not receive the same press from Jesus as He gave to the sheep:

> 'But then the King will say to the goats on His left, "Go away from Me into the eternal fire made ready for the devil and his angels, for you are cursed. I was hungry but you gave Me nothing, I was thirsty and you didn't care. I was a stranger and you ignored Me. I was cold and you gave Me nothing to wear. I was sick and in prison and you avoided Me."
>
> Then the goats will answer, "Lord when did we see you hungry or thirsty or as a stranger or cold, sick or in prison, and did nothing to help you?"' (Matt. 25:41-44)

Their attitude seems to be that they would have done something to help if they had realised that the Lord was involved in all this suffering. But in effect they were too wrapped up in themselves, in their own desires and needs, to be concerned for others. Perhaps some of them regarded themselves as sheep, whereas Jesus sees them as goats! And what is His judgment on them?

> 'The King will reply, "I tell you the truth, when you failed to do any of these things for other people who I regard as My brothers, you refused to do them for Me."
>
> Then the goats will suffer eternal punishment, but the righteous sheep will enjoy eternal life.' (Matt. 26:45-46)

This is the telling phrase: '*Whatever you did not do for one of the least of these, you did not do for me.*' This reminds us of what John said:

> 'Whoever claims to live in Him has to demonstrate this by walking as Jesus did.' (1 John 2:6)

And Jesus constantly gave Himself to others as the Servant He came to be.

The One who lives in you is the One who came to serve, and He wants to give Himself to others through you. It is a mistake to think that God sent His Son to save us so that we can go to heaven. No, He saved us to enable us to fulfil His will on earth, and then we can go to heaven! This is why He taught us to pray:

> *'May your Kingdom come and your will be done on earth as is already the case in heaven.' (Matt. 6:10)*

We all need servant hearts, like the heart of our Lord and Master. Then we will want to serve others by loving them in the same way that Jesus has loved us, in fulfilment of His command:

> *'As I have loved you, so you must love one another.' (John 13:34)*

He has placed His love within us to enable this. The word used for God's love in the original Greek means a love that is expressed in positive action. It is not a love based on emotion or physical attraction. In fact God's love in us can enable us to love effectively those for whom we have no emotional feelings, and even those who would never attract us in the natural. His love enables us to love those who have never known true love and may deliberately make it difficult for others to love them, because they want to try to prove that it is impossible for anyone to love them, even God! This shows how their view of themselves is very negative; and yet there are many such people in the world all around us.

The Lord does not need a people who will only speak of His love, but who will demonstrate the value of that love by their actions. So overused is the word 'love' in our modern society that it is almost impossible for a non-believer to understand what is meant by a Christian saying: "God loves you." This is why John writes;

'Dear children, it means nothing to say you love others; it is only your actions that show whether you truly love them or not.' (1 John 3:18)

Words without the right actions are meaningless. Our message is to be seen in what we do in the Name of Jesus Christ as He works through us.

When a person becomes a new believer he does not know how to live as a Christian. He will inevitably do what he sees other believers doing. He learns from example, more than from being told what to do.

As the church our commission is to make disciples. From the gospels we see how Jesus Himself went about this task. He not only taught His disciples, He demonstrated His love and power in action and then sent them out with the message of God's Kingdom, but also to do the same works of the Kingdom. Likewise Paul could encourage the church, *'Just as I follow Christ's example, I suggest you follow mine'* (1 Cor. 11:1). This shows what a responsibility Christian leaders have. The writer to Hebrews says:

'Remember to honour your leaders and to pray for them. They have spoken God's Word to you. You can see from their example that they live their message and they demonstrate how to walk by faith. Jesus Christ is the same today as He has been in the past, and He will always remain the same for all eternity.' (Heb. 13:7-8)

Leaders have the responsibility to teach God's Word, but also to demonstrate what they teach by the way they live. They are to live by faith as well as teach faith, so that others can imitate their faith, to see how faith operates in action, demonstrating that Jesus Christ is the same yesterday, today and forever!

How can leaders live up to such expectations unless Christ is being revealed through their lives and ministries? In reality it is the way in which they allow the Christ within them to flow out of them that makes them genuine spiritual leaders. These are the leaders who will make disciples and show others how they too can become leaders.

How can a leader or any other believer demonstrate that Jesus Christ is the same yesterday, today and forever unless he allows the Christ who lives within him to be manifested through him, both by the way he speaks and the things he does? The answer lies in the nature and heart-attitude of the believer. If he wants to please himself he will do what he desires rather than what the Lord wants him to do. In the case of the leader, he will use his natural gifts and powers of persuasion, rather than allow the Head of the Church to lead through him.

The leader who trusts in the Christ within will be a person able to exercise the Lord's authority. The leader who trusts in himself will be authoritarian. He will seek to lord it over people, the very thing Jesus warned against!

When the Lord's true authority is exercised, people sense that the Lord is really in charge. The leadership of the church is truly submitted to His authority and so the whole body of believers can benefit. They will lead by example, with authority and in love. They will be neither legalistic on the one hand nor liberal on the other hand. They will speak and live the truth so that people see how to live in the true liberty of the Spirit.

CHAPTER 6

THE AUTHORITY OF CHRIST IN YOUR LIFE

Every believer is to exercise the authority of Christ – over temptation and sin, over all the power of the evil one, in commanding mountains to be moved through prayer, in speaking the will of God into being.

The key to being able to exercise the authority given us by Christ is to be submitted and fully yielded to the authority of Christ. This is easy to say, but has to be worked out in practice if we are to be the men and women of authority and power that God has called us to be. In this we have the example that Jesus gave during His ministry on earth.

The authority of Christ Jesus

Jesus was the Man of authority. '*He spoke with great authority, not at all like the teachers of the law they were accustomed to hearing.*' (Matt. 7:29) Even His opponents recognised that He spoke and acted with authority. They asked Him, "Where did you get that authority?" "Who gave you this authority to do the these things?"

What was the secret of His authority? He was fully submitted and yielded to the authority of His Father in heaven. He said: '*To see Me is to see the Father. So why ask Me to show you the Father. Simply believe that I am in the Father and that the Father is in Me.*' (John 14:9-10)

He made it clear that in His manhood He could do nothing of Himself:

> '*Jesus continued: "I tell you the truth, the Son is incapable of doing anything on His own; He can do only what He sees His Father doing. Whatever the Father does, His Son also does."*' (*John 5:19*)

This is the Son of God saying that He could do nothing independently of the Father. He could do only what He saw the Father doing. Jesus had to remain at one with the Father, fully submitted to His will. *"The work I am doing is what My Father is giving Me to do."* (John 5:36)

He then taught His disciples: *"Anyone who continues to live in Me and I in him will be abundantly fruitful. But outside of Me you can do absolutely nothing"*. (John 15:5) Just as Jesus could do nothing apart from the Father, so we can do nothing apart from Jesus Christ.

Our experience may contradict this, for we could say there are many things we can do in our own strength and with our own natural abilities. It would seem that Jesus indicates that all such activity is worth nothing in God's eyes, because it cannot produce fruit that will last.

Jesus was the Word of God that became man and lived on earth; yet He said: *"So you can be sure that I only say what the Father has commanded Me to say."* (John 12:49) Just as He would not do anything independently of His Father, so He would not say anything independently of Him. So Jesus lived in complete submission to His Father, speaking what He gave Him to speak, doing what He saw Him doing, fulfilling the Father's will and not His own.

Clearly Jesus had a will of His own or He would not have shared in our humanity completely. He submitted His will to that of His Father at all times, and taught His disciples to do likewise. Even though He was the Son of God, He refused to act independently of the Father's authority.

Because He was submitted to authority He could exercise His Father's authority. If you are submitted to the authority of Jesus Christ then you can exercise His authority. You can speak and act in His name, on His behalf. How does this work in practice? 'Not I, but Christ!'

Christ's authority in us

We submit to God by refusing to trust in our own strength, or to take the initiative into our own hands. We allow the Christ in us to work through us.

I cannot; but you can.

I will not; so you will!

We refuse to act impulsively or in self-dependence.

It is not only the way we act that determines how truly we are submitted to God's will. Our submission is seen in the way we react to situations. When hurt by others, do we forgive or do we retaliate or take offence? When we have given of ourselves in loving service are we looking for appreciation and thanks, or do we believe what Jesus says, that even when we have done everything we should, we are still unprofitable servants?

When confronted with a need, do we respond in love, or do we avoid the issue, especially if it seems costly to respond? Do we want to put God's Word into practice or are we content to draw on His life only for ourselves?

Again it is a matter of the heart as to how we answer such questions as these. **Disciples are those who place Christ first, before themselves, their family members, their own desires. In this way they will prosper, as will their families and those around them, whose lives they will touch with the life and power of Christ.**

We need to exercise authority over all the ways the devil and his demonic forces come against us. How do we do this?

> *'So submit yourselves wholeheartedly to God, stand against*
> *the devil and he will run from you.' (James 4:7)*

Many omit the first part of this verse, but it is essential to the whole process. For when I submit to the Lord's authority then He will exercise His authority through me! **Without that submission I am fighting on my own. With that submission Christ in me comes against the enemy and he flees, for he has no answer to such authority!**

If I live submitted to Christ then when the enemy attacks me, he will come up against the One to whom I am submitted, the One who has already overcome Him on the cross.

Submission is outworked in obedience. A submitted heart is an obedient heart. Jesus said:

> *'"Who really loves Me? The one who not only has My com-*
> *mands but obeys them! Anyone who genuinely loves Me*
> *like that will be loved by My Father. I will also love him*
> *and will continue to reveal Myself to him."' (John 14:21)*

So obedience is ultimately the outward expression of our love for Jesus Christ. He expressed His love for the Father by obeying Him and doing His will. **We express our love for Jesus by obeying Him and doing His will.** And in obeying Him, we obey the Father also. Jesus said:

> *'You will remain in My love, if you obey what I have commanded you, in the same way that I have remained in My Father's love by obeying what He commanded Me. I have told you this because I want you to have within you the same joy that is in Me. I want you to be absolutely full of joy.' (John 15:10-11)*

This is the joyful way in which we live, in obedience to His will! In this way we remain in His love and we are filled with His joy. To go against His will puts us in a place of tension in our relationship with the Lord, and we then lose our peace and joy. **A loving heart is a submitted heart, an obedient heart!**

Because He is Lord, Jesus always commanded or told the disciples what to do, for the way He exercised His authority was by command. He did not ask His disciples if they minded doing this or that, nor was He issuing useful hints on how to live a good life. He commanded! Always with love; nevertheless He commanded. And it is for us to obey His commands.

And this is why He lives with us, to enable us to obey and so fulfil His will and do what pleases Him. John writes:

> *'My dear friends, if there is nothing in our hearts to make us feel condemned, we can have confidence before God when we pray, and so are able to receive from Him anything we ask. This is because we are living in obedience to His commands and are doing what pleases Him. And this is His command, as you know well: first to believe that Jesus Christ is God's Son, your Saviour and Lord, and then that you love others and allow them to love you as He has commanded us. Those who obey His commands show they continue to live in Him, and He lives in them. We can be sure that He does live in us because He has given us His Spirit.' (1 John 3:21-24)*

So we see there are a number of great advantages to living in obedience to Jesus Christ:

- We are able to exercise His authority.
- We can resist the devil and he will flee.
- We will remain in the love of Jesus.
- We will be filled with His joy.
- We will receive from Him whatever we ask in prayer.
- We will continue to live in Him.
- He will continue to live in us!

Seven good reasons to obey! But the most compelling reason of all is that we demonstrate our love for Him by obeying Him. And His command is to love others, to allow the life of Christ who lives within us to flow out of us and to touch the lives of all those around us, whether they be members of our families, our churches, our neighbours, those with whom we work, or even casual acquaintances.

The Lord is looking for consistency in this, that we do not limit ourselves to the occasional denying of ourselves and submission of our will, but that this becomes our way of life!

Again, it is a matter of heart attitude. Are we living for ourselves, or for Christ Jesus and therefore for others? The truth is that we do not live for Him unless we live for others. Of course this will be costly, but not to the Christ in us. The cost is only to our flesh, that self-life that would always like to have its own way!

The rewards for obedience far outweigh the cost. John points out that His commands are not a burden. This is certainly true when we are motivated by love for Christ Jesus and for others. Commands only become a burden when we fight against God's will for us because we want to please ourselves rather than Him.

I can look back on many years of serving the Lord by loving and serving others, and can testify that it is a tremendously rewarding and fulfilling way to live. When it has been demanding, His grace has always been sufficient. When I have felt incapable (and that has been often) His power has been made perfect in my weakness!

I can at least say that I have sought to please the Lord and can only be thankful for the ways in which so many people's lives have been impacted by

Christ working through me. And most definitely all the glory for that belongs to Him. For it is, 'Not I, but Christ!'

CHAPTER 7

CLOTHED WITH CHRIST

Paul writes:

> *'For all of you are made sons of God through faith in Christ Jesus. All those who have been baptised into Christ have been clothed with Christ.' (Gal. 3:26-27)*

As soon as we have come to faith in Christ Jesus we are to be baptised in water. That is the scriptural position. We are not baptised into the church, but into Christ Jesus. We become participators of His life and He lives in us to work through us.

By choosing to be baptised as believers we have also clothed ourselves with Christ! **So you live in Christ Jesus, He lives in you and you have clothed yourself with Him.** Truly you are one with Him! Elsewhere Paul says:

> *'You will radiate the life of the Lord Jesus Christ, living as His witness. How much better to have that as your aim than to live to gratify your fleshly, self-indulgent desires!' (Rom. 13:14)*

We have to allow Christ within us to express Himself through our lives; we also have to make the conscious decision to clothe ourselves with Christ.

When speaking about this subject I like to put on a cloak that goes from my shoulders to my ankles and that I can wrap around me completely. I explain that the cloak represents Christ. Beneath the cloak is the weak Colin, but I have clothed myself with the One who is the strength of my life. Whatever comes against me actually comes against Him. He is a shield about me.

So there is no better way to stay protected from whatever comes against me either directly from the enemy, or his actions through other people!

However, there is another positive reason for living clothed with Christ. People will see Him, rather than you. He will be seen in what you do, in the way you act and react, and in the attitudes you display when responding to the challenges that confront you.

Our weakness does not matter if we are clothed with Christ. And we can consciously 'put on' whatever aspects of His life are necessary in the particular circumstances in which we find ourselves.

> *'So I speak to you as God's chosen people. You are holy, set apart by God to belong to Him as His own children. You are dearly loved by Him and can clothe yourselves with compassion, kindness, humility, gentleness and patience. Yes, be patient with one another and forgive any differences that arise between you. Forgive as the Lord forgave you, no matter how deeply hurt you feel.*
>
> *The highest virtue is love, for this keeps all these other qualities in their right place and enables you to live in unity with others.' (Col. 3:12-14)*

Because we are clothed with Christ it is His compassion we put on. This is not simply feeling sorry for people, which is merely an emotion of our own souls.

When Jesus had compassion on people, He was always moved to action! In compassion He forgave sins, as with the woman caught in the act of adultery. When He saw the crowds they appeared like sheep without a shepherd; so He had compassion on them and taught them. When He healed the sick, it was the outworking of the compassion He had for them. He is 'full of compassion and mercy!' (James 5:11)

So with Christ in us and because we are clothed with Christ, we are to see others as He sees them, with His eyes, and a heart of compassion that will move us to appropriate action! It is His compassion that is to flow from our lives to others!

In like manner, Paul is not speaking of human kindness, but of the kindness which is the fruit of the Spirit within us. If we have the kindness of

Christ within us, we are to be clothed with that kindness so that it shows in the positive actions we perform!

You have the humility of Christ within you, even though your self-life remains proud. What you want others to see is not your personal selfishness, but the humility of Christ.

> *'And do not be conceited for that is only empty vanity. Rather, live humbly, thinking that others are better than yourselves. Yes, you will have to be responsible about your own affairs, but you should be equally concerned about the interests of others around you. In fact your attitude should reflect that of Christ Jesus Himself.*
>
> *By nature He is God, but He did not hold onto His divine status of being equal with the Father in heaven. He was prepared to make Himself nothing, taking the nature of a servant and becoming thoroughly human. He was a man in every respect, even though He retained His divinity. Even so, He humbled Himself to such an extent that He obeyed the Father's will that He should die the death of a criminal on the cross.'* (Phil. 2:3-8)

With Christ in us and being clothed with Christ our attitude is to be the same as His! Do you now understand? **Your self-life, your flesh, will never have that same attitude but, as you give way to Christ in you, so then that same attitude can be expressed in your life.** Others will see the humility of Christ in you. Peter writes:

> *'The young men among you must be submissive to those who are older. All of you are to clothe yourselves with humility towards each other because, "God opposes proud people but gives His grace freely to the humble."'* (1 Peter 5:5-6)

Christ is your life, your righteousness, your holiness, your humility. Here again is a command to all believers: 'Clothe yourselves with humility towards one another'. The humility of Christ who lives within you!

It is not a matter of trying to be humble, but allowing the humility of the One who lives in you to be expressed. There are bound to be occasions when you will be conscious of your pride. **Instead of fighting against yourself, submit yourself to Christ and say: 'Lord, let your humility come forth now, for I am so full of pride myself.'** And He will do that. Instead of speaking or acting with pride, He will give you the grace to be humble!

Gentleness and patience are also fruit of the Spirit of Christ who lives in you. So Paul says that you are also to clothe yourselves with these qualities.

We rightly think of Jesus as the Man of great authority and power. And yet He described His own heart in this way:

> *'Be united with Me and learn from Me, for I have a humble*
> *and gentle heart; then you will find peace for your souls.'*
> *(Matt. 11:29)*

Here Jesus links gentleness and humility and says these describe the nature of His heart. This is the heart of Christ who lives in you. He is both gentle and humble, but still full of power and authority. **He lives in us; we are clothed with Him and are also yoked together with Him!**

People can hear what we say when we speak with gentleness, not harsh judgmentalism. You can hear the Holy Spirit in a prophetic word that is brought with gentleness and humility. But you hear only the speaker when he addresses the people in a rough and strident manner. The Spirit of Christ is both gentle and humble, even though He is the authority and power of God within us!

Love is expressed in gentleness. This is not a sign of weakness, but of the strength of Christ working through us! When dealing with others we must always remember that they are like us in that they can be easily and unnecessarily hurt by harsh attitudes.

Patience and gentleness go well together! The flesh, your self-life, tends to be impatient, especially when you do not get your own way, or things do not turn out as you wanted. Impatience leads to bad temper, and that is not only self-destructive but causes harm to those around us. **Within you is the patience of Christ!** Paul encourages his readers:

> *'We want you to live lives worthy of the Lord so that you*
> *will please Him in every way possible. For you will produce*
> *much fruit for His glory, through all His good works you*
> *do as you continue to know Him better. He strengthens*
> *you with all the power of His glorious might, and it is this*
> *power in you that gives you patience, enables you to persist*
> *in doing His will and causes you to maintain your joy,*
> *thanking God the Father for all He has done in you.' (Col.*
> *1:10-12)*

Christ's power within you will give you patience, when you trust in Him and not yourself.

Some people pray for more patience when they already have the life of Christ with them. **He is your patience, as He is your humility and gentleness!**

Is everything becoming clearer to you? Within you is every dimension of the life of Christ, and you can choose to clothe yourself with every dimension of His life. Then Christ will be seen in you instead of the harsh, proud, impatient self! Yes, we all have to learn to depend on Him, to defer to Him, so that His life will radiate from our lives. We have to learn to give way to Him. 'Not I, but Christ in me.'

If we clothe ourselves with Christ, we are also clothed with forgiveness towards those who grieve us in any way. It is inevitable that others will upset us and offend us from time to time. There may be occasions when you have to work through a situation in which someone causes you continual grievance. What are you to do in such circumstances? Forgive and continue to forgive, to have a heart attitude of mercy, even if the other person does not repent of the harm he or she is causing you. It helps to remember how the Lord is continually merciful towards you, every morning, and that He has had to forgive you frequently! If we are clothed with Christ, we are clothed with mercy. Jesus said:

> *'The merciful are blessed, for God will be merciful to them.'*
> *(Matt. 5:7)*

And if we do not forgive others, then our Father in heaven will not forgive us (see Matt. 6:14-15). That in itself should give us sufficient motivation always to forgive.

However, we have another good reason for doing so: we want the Lord of mercy, the Lord Jesus Christ, to be expressed through us. And when we fail to forgive we are not at peace with Him!

In the parable Jesus taught, the unmerciful servant was *'turned over to the jailers to be tortured, until he should pay back all he owed.'* (Matt. 18:15-35) We torture ourselves when we refuse to forgive others. We add to the burden we already feel by being grieved or hurt. Jesus concluded the parable by warning:

> *'This is how My heavenly Father will deal with you unless you are merciful and forgive your brother from your heart.'*
> *(Matt. 18:35)*

He would not have issued such a dire warning unless He knew how important it is to forgive. We cannot have relationship with God until we have been forgiven, and it is obvious that if we fail to forgive others, this places an immediate and serious strain on our relationship with Him!

> *'The highest virtue is love, for this keeps all these other qualities in their right place and enables you to live in unity with others.' (Col. 3:14)*

To be clothed with Christ, Paul writes, is to be clothed with compassion, kindness, humility, gentleness, patience, forgiveness, and, of course, with love which binds all these qualities together so we reveal that Christ is living within us.

This is God's love, not our human emotional love. It is the love that is expressed in giving ourselves wholeheartedly to Him and to others. **It is the love that is revealed through serving Him and others. It is the love of positive action.**

'His love in us enables us to be patient and kind. When motivated by this love we do not envy others, neither do we boast. Nor are we proud!

God's love in us is not rude, nor self seeking. We are not roused to anger quickly and we certainly do not keep a mental record of the wrongs others have committed. When God's love works through us we take no delight in what He regards as evil. Rather we rejoice in the truth that sets people free from evil. Those who truly love always protect others, they always trust, are always full of hope. They always persevere, regardless of the circumstances.

So love never fails to accomplish its objectives.' (1 Cor. 13:4-8)

Do not think that such love is beyond you. **This is the nature of the love God has already placed within you when He poured His Holy Spirit into your heart.** So you can clothe yourself with His love.

In your natural self-life you cannot possibly love like that. To try to do so would end in failure again and again. But if instead of trying in your own strength you yield yourself to Christ, then He can express His love through you.

There will be many occasions when you will have all kinds of negative emotions and thoughts. Yet when you trust Him, His love comes through in what you say and do, instead of those negative reactions. And as soon as this begins to happen your emotions and attitudes change.

I never cease to be amazed at the way the amazing love of Jesus is expressed when I am dealing with difficult situations. When you begin to express this love, you become caught up in it yourself and sense the tremendous love, compassion and mercy that God has for the person you are dealing with.

God has put the life of His Son within you, but it is for you to make the conscious decision to clothe yourself with Christ. He is your defence and shield, and you will radiate His life and glory.

CHAPTER 8

THE KINGDOM WITHIN YOU

Jesus came with the gospel of the Kingdom of God or the Kingdom of heaven. In scripture the word translated 'kingdom' means, 'kingly rule' or 'reign'. If Christ Jesus lives within you He has established His kingly rule and reign in your heart and life.

> 'Some Pharisees asked Jesus when God's Kingdom would come. He answered them: "God's Kingdom does not come by looking for it, neither will you be able to say, 'It is here', or 'It is over there.' For God's Kingdom is within you."'
> (Luke 17:20-21)

If the King is within you, His Kingdom is within you, His kingly rule and reign is within you.

In His ministry we can see how Jesus reigned over sin, over sickness, over the devil, over His circumstances. He exercised His reign and therefore His authority over demonic forces. Nothing could overcome Him.

On several occasions His opponents wanted to kill Him, but they were unable to do so. He could only be arrested when He gave Himself willingly into the hands of His captors. Even then they fell before the glory that radiated from Him; so He could have walked away freely if He had chosen to do that. Alternatively, He could have called on His Father to send legions of angels to rescue Him. He had the power to lay down His life and to take it up again.

What does it mean for you to have the Kingdom or the kingly rule of God in your life? Three things:

1. Christ Jesus wants to rule over you.
2. Christ Jesus wants to reign in you.
3. Christ Jesus wants to exercise His kingly rule and reign through you.

1. His rule over us

It is obvious that because He is Lord, Jesus Christ is the ultimate authority. It is not for us to try to manipulate God into doing what we want Him to do; but we are to be submitted to Him to see His will for our lives fulfilled.

He reigns over us in love and with wisdom; He never forces us to do His will. He commands us because He is Lord and then awaits our obedience, an obedience that is the expression of our love for Him. It is impossible to force love; it has to be a willing response to His love for us!

To say that we willingly place ourselves under the sovereign reign of the Lord Jesus Christ is to say that we place ourselves under the authority of His Word. Remember that Jesus is the Word of God that was sent from heaven to live among us. There can be no higher authority than that of the scriptures. This is a much higher authority than the books of other religions because the New Testament records the words and actions of God's Son, and every part of it is inspired by His Spirit.

We can determine whether we are living in the truth or not by seeing whether His Word is being expressed in our lives. To live by faith is to put God's Word into action! To place ourselves under the authority of the Word is to put what God says into action. We do not merely read or listen to what the scriptures say. **We do the Word!**

However, we are not trying to obey the Word in our own strength. We saw how the people of Israel were unable to obey God's law because they did not possess the inner power that enabled them to do so. But we have received the life and power of the Holy Spirit, the Spirit of Christ. Jesus promised:

> *'However, you will receive God's power when you are bap-*
> *tised in the Holy Spirit. Then you will be My witnesses in*
> *Jerusalem, the whole of Judea and Samaria and in every*
> *part of the earth.' (Acts 1:8)*

The Spirit of God and the Word of God always agree together. Jesus said little about the Holy Spirit until the Last Supper. He then put the focus on the fact that He is the Spirit of Truth who guides us into all the truth.

> *'To enable this obedience, when I return to heaven I will ask*
> *the Father to replace Me with another Counsellor exactly*

like Me, who will remain with you forever. He is the Spirit
of Truth.' (John 14:16)

The word translated 'another' here means, 'another of exactly the same kind'! There are only two counsellors in scripture. The first is the 'Wonderful Counsellor', referring to Jesus Christ. The other is the Holy Spirit who is of exactly the same kind as Jesus. So the Spirit of Christ who lives within you is your Counsellor, just as Jesus was the Wonderful Counsellor. It is not surprising, therefore, that the Holy Spirit does not want you to do anything independently of Jesus, but to keep your focus on Him.

'I have told you all these things while I am still with you.
The Father will send you the Counsellor, the Holy Spirit, in
My Name. When He comes He will teach you all you need
to know and will remind you of everything I have already
taught you.' (John 14:26)

Why should He do this? So that we can obey everything Jesus said!

When giving His commission to His church through the original apostles, Jesus told them that they were to go and make disciples of all nations, baptising people in the name of the Father, Son and Holy Spirit. They were also to **'teach them to obey everything I have taught and commanded you.'** (Matt. 28:20)

So we are to obey everything Jesus commanded His first disciples to do. And He has placed His own Spirit within us to enable this. How far each believer obeys is determined to what extent he or she is truly submitted to the kingly rule of Jesus Christ in his or her life. Jesus asked:

'Why do you say to Me, 'Lord, Lord,' and yet you do not put
what I say into practice?' (Luke 6:46)

It makes no sense to say that Jesus is Lord of your life and yet you live in disobedience to His Word, and therefore to His will. Jesus also warned:

'Because someone says to Me, 'Lord, Lord,' does not mean
he or she will necessarily enter the Kingdom of heaven; that

is reserved for those who do the will of My Father who is in
heaven.' (Matt. 7:21)

Disobedience is not an option. The Christ within you cannot be revealed through sin or disobedience! Because the Holy Spirit will guide us into all the truth, we are to obey Him by learning to follow His leading in our lives.

> *'The Holy Spirit will glorify Me because He will take hold*
> *of all I have said and done, and will reveal it to you. Every-*
> *thing that the Father has, I also have. And everything I*
> *have the Spirit will take and reveal to you in your experi-*
> *ence.' (John 16:13-14)*

The Holy Spirit will remind you of everything Jesus said. And He will only speak what Jesus and the Father tell Him to speak to you. The whole Trinity of God functions in complete unity.

This is the ministry the Holy Spirit fulfils within you for the Father's glory, empowering you to please Him. Paul says that *'those who are led by the Spirit of God are sons of God.'* (Rom. 8:14) **The sons of God will live for His glory by obeying His will, by allowing the Lord Jesus Christ to exercise His kingly rule over them.** They are happy to obey Him out of love for Him! They are happy to submit to His Lordship and therefore to His authority, to His will as expressed in God's Word. And the Spirit of Christ lives within believers to enable this whole process! Jesus made this amazing statement, that everything the Father, the Son and the Holy Spirit have is yours! (John 16:15)

Think what this means. The Holy Spirit makes known in your experience everything that belongs to the Father and the Son. This is amazing!

It proves that God does not expect you to obey Him in your own strength, by dependence on your natural abilities. He says that nothing good dwells in that self-life. He knows there will be times when you will have no natural desire to obey, that you will have to deny yourself to do so.

Instead you have been given the fullness of Christ to live within you. You have been given everything you need for life and godliness. You live in God and He lives in you. And the Holy Spirit will guide you into all truth

and has given you the power that enables the Christ who is in you to be expressed through you.

The more you allow Christ to reign over you, the more His reign will be expressed in your life in practice. Others will be blessed and the Father glorified in your life.

2. His reign in you

It should be obvious from all this that the measure that Christ is allowed to reign in your life is determined by the degree to which you allow Him to rule *over* your life. **The more you are submitted to Him, the more He can exercise His reign in your life.** The more He does that, the more you will benefit personally. For this means you will be able to reign over sin and temptation, over the devil and all his works, and over adverse circumstances whenever they afflict you.

So, for example, you will reign over sickness if it attacks your body, over negative thoughts or negative feelings about yourself! Because you live under the authority of Christ you will be able to exercise His authority. His reign will be expressed in your life. Jesus said:

> *'Have faith in God. I tell you most emphatically, if anyone speaks to a mountain by saying, 'Go, throw yourself into the sea,' the mountain will be moved for him so long as he does not doubt in his heart, but truly believes that what he says must happen.' (Mark 11:22-23)*

We have seen that the Lord Jesus exercised His authority by issuing commands. It is interesting to note that when He did so the demons always obeyed, but human beings did not always do so! This was true even of His disciples. The demons had to obey; they could not withstand His authority.

However, because God will not interfere with our free will, our ability to make decisions, we all have the choice as to whether to obey out of love for Him, or disobey out of love for ourselves!

Jesus is teaching His disciples here that His authority in their lives will also be expressed in the issuing of commands, even when they pray. Like Jesus, you can use your authority against the forces of the enemy and expect obedience, but you cannot force other people to obey God. Some church leaders mistakingly try to do so, but this only leads to legalism and bondage.

How effective we are in commanding with authority is dependent on our faith in God; that we believe we have the authority and power of the Kingdom that He has given us, that we believe the risen Christ can exercise His authority and power through us as we speak and act in His name.

To say that His Kingdom is within you is to say that His kingly rule and authority are within you, and can be expressed when you speak or act in His Name. You can command the mountains, the obstacles that confront you, to be removed. If you are living under Christ's authority, you do not need to live under oppression or anything sent by the enemy in an attempt to distract you away from God's purposes.

Many make the mistake of praying about their problems rather than addressing them and commanding them to be moved. Where there is faith, believers will address their problems or needs and command them to be removed.

There is no formula for doing this, as Jesus says it is a matter of exercising the faith that is in the heart of the one praying. **We are given authority by Jesus to pray in His Name, in His Person. When we do this, the authority of Christ within us is in the prayer, and so things happen as a result.** It is not a matter of only using the name of Jesus, but praying what He would pray with the faith and expectation He would have.

Again, the Holy Spirit will enable us to do this, for Paul says the Holy Spirit helps us in our weakness when we do not know how to pray. He will show us what to believe, and what to say when we pray. Remember, you exercise authority by commanding things to happen. You are to command the problems, the mountains of need, to be removed, with the expectation that your commands will be obeyed!

Remember that God's purpose is for you to overcome, to conquer, to be victorious. You will only be able to do that by exercising the authority of Christ within you to enable you to overcome your circumstances.

The promises the Holy Spirit gives to the seven churches in Revelation, chapters two and three, are addressed to those who overcome. So He will certainly be at work within you to enable you to overcome. He even promises:

'To Him who is victorious, who keeps My ways until the end, I will give authority over the nations, just as I received authority from My Father. "He will shepherd them with an iron rod that breaks clay pots into pieces." I will also give the morning star, Myself, to everyone who is victorious.' (Rev. 2:26-27)

3. His reign through you

It must be remembered that you are not expressing an authority of your own, but His authority in you. All authority belongs to the Lord, but He has chosen to delegate that authority to those who live in Him and in whom He lives. **You speak, with His authority whenever you speak what He gives you to say!** And you can be confident that His words spoken through you will produce life in others, because the life is in the Word, not in the voice that speaks it!

His authority will be expressed whenever you act in obedience to His Word and Spirit.

When listening to people preach, you can tell when they speak with authority, not only by the way they speak, but because of the content of what they say. This is why Jesus' opponents recognised that He spoke with authority, even though they did not like what He said! There is something compelling about the truth when spoken under the authority of the Holy Spirit.

Likewise, when we act with authority there is a confidence and boldness about what we do, even though we may feel neither confident nor bold in ourselves. It is the work of Christ within us. Denying yourself will often involve denying the negative thoughts and feelings of that self-life.

When we pray with others we should not use many words. Jesus warns us against such prayer. No, like Him, we should speak and pray with authority. Our commission is to heal the sick, not simply to pray for them. Again this is a matter of what you believe in your heart. The Lord wants us to understand that we are exercising His authority, acting in His Name under the authority of His Spirit, in obedience to His Word. It is all a matter of Christ working through us.

He wants you to believe that because He lives in you, it is His will for you to be a channel of His grace and power to others. Then the life of Christ

will flow through you and into those for when you pray, and to whom you minister in His Name!

Once you realise that He will use you in this way, you welcome the opportunity to be a channel of His grace and power to others. Often you will marvel at what He does, even though you may feel very weak and even incompetent in yourself. All the glory belongs to Him, for this is Christ in you working through you for the Father's glory and the benefit of His people.

At the same time you are revealing the presence of God's Kingdom. **His Kingdom life, authority and power are to be revealed through you!** Paul says:

> *'This is the confidence we have before God through our faith in Christ. We are not able, because of our natural abilities, to claim any credit for ourselves. Our ability comes from God. He has made us able to be ministers of the new covenant, which is based not on the letter of the law, but on the Spirit of God. For religious legalism kills, but God's Spirit gives life!' (2 Cor. 3:4-6)*

We are not competent in ourselves, but our competence comes from the Spirit of Christ within us. And no one is more competent than Him!

Jesus taught the disciples about the Kingdom of God and then sent them out to preach about the Kingdom and to perform the signs and wonders that verified their message that the Kingdom was now present among men.

A church congregation is to be a group of born again, Spirit-filled people who belong to the Kingdom. The Kingdom is within them and they proclaim the good news of the Kingdom and perform the signs and wonders of the Kingdom in the Name of Jesus. This is what makes congregational life exciting, because others outside the church are being impacted by the life and power of the Kingdom because of the way Christ works through His people.

In this way the sovereign reign of Christ is extended within the lives of more and more people; Christ reigning through His people to extend His reign into the lives of other people.

Whatever God does always has a 'so that' attached to it. He does everything with purpose. **He lives within you so that He can extend His Kingdom** through you. What a privilege, to be part of God's eternal purposes! He reigns over you, in you and through you. No wonder Jesus says:

> *'Let the Kingdom of heaven and living in a right relation-*
> *ship with God be your priorities; then everything else you*
> *need will be given to you as well.'* *(Matt. 6:33)*

By His grace, the Kingdom of God is within you. Jesus Christ is your righteousness, and so you have no worries, for the Lord will look after every need that could arise in your life, which is why Jesus says: '***Do not worry about your life.***' (Matt. 6:25) That, too, is a command, not a piece of advice!

What have we to worry about with His assurance that He will take care of every need if we keep our focus on the work of His Kingdom?

CHAPTER 9

HE IS YOUR SALVATION AND HEALTH

We have seen that because the righteous One lives in us He has become our righteousness. We do not need to try and acquire a righteousness of our own. He is Holy, and so He is our holiness. He is our Saviour, and so is our salvation!

Some people are concerned about whether a person can lose his or her salvation. It needs to be remembered that in scripture salvation is a process. **The believer has been saved, is being saved, and expects to be saved on the Day of Judgment.**

Salvation is also the Person of Christ Jesus Himself. God is concerned that we continue to live in union and fellowship with Him through our Lord Jesus Christ.

Because Christ is in you, He is your salvation. As you continue to walk with Him, so you continue to live in His saving grace.

Salvation is a relationship with Jesus Christ, God's gift to us. He has saved us from our past, from sin and failure, from our inability to please Him. He has saved us from falling into temptation and living under the power and influence of the evil one. He has saved us from the fear of death and a Christ-less eternity.

He has saved us for Himself, for His Kingdom purposes, to fulfil the plan He has for each believer's life. He has saved us to reveal the presence and power of Christ through our lives. He has saved us to make His Kingdom available to others through our witness and obedience to Him.

'My dear friends, you see why it has been so important for you to obey the Lord, not only when I am with you but even more when we are apart. Continue to live as those who are saved, who fear the Lord, dreading the idea of ever denying Him. For God Himself is at work within you so that you want to do what is good in His eyes.' (Phil. 2:12-13)

It is a great comfort to know that it is the Lord Himself who lives in us to enable the outworking of 'His good purpose.' You can see from several scriptures already quoted, how important it is to live a life of obedience to God. In our own strength that would be impossible; it is made possible by Christ being in us!

However, we still need the will to obey, and the willingness to deny ourselves and trust in Him instead. 'Not I, but Christ in me!'

By living the saved life you will become an influence on others that will lead them to salvation. Your example of obedience will be a good witness to those you influence. Who we are is as important as the things we do, for we want others to see Christ in us, as well as receive Him through us.

Our healer and our healing

The Greek word for 'save' can also be translated 'heal'! So we can see that salvation and healing are very closely connected. It is possible to translate Jesus' words as 'your faith has saved you' or, 'your faith has healed you.'

You could say that full salvation is full healing of spirit, soul and body. Jesus made such full salvation possible and available through the cross. He died to save us from sickness, infirmity and affliction as well as from sin, transgressions and iniquity. He was even crushed to save us from all that has a crushing effect on our lives, as Isaiah 53 makes clear. Whatever negative we can experience He took upon Himself so that we could be set free. This is why Paul says:

> *'Christ has set us free to live in freedom. So stand fast in that freedom and do not allow yourselves to be yoked again in slavery.*
>
> *Listen carefully: I, Paul, tell you clearly that if you allow yourselves to become legalistically religious again, Christ will be of no value to you. I say it again to everyone, if you have become legalistic you are obligated to obey every aspect of the religious law. For those of you who are trying to make yourselves acceptable through obeying the religious code have become separated from Christ; you have deserted the*

life of grace. For it is by the Spirit that we eagerly await the hope of our eternal acceptance by faith. For in Christ Jesus neither being a Jew or a Gentile is of any significance; all that matters is that you live a life of faith that is expressed in a life of love for God and others.

You were making such good progress. So who is now preventing you from obeying the truth? This certainly is not the influence of the One who has called you. A little yeast soon affects the whole lump of dough!

In the Lord I have confidence in you, that you will not be side-tracked. Anyone who tries to influence you in that way will certainly be judged, no matter who he may be. Brothers, if I am still preaching conformity to the religious law, why am I still being persecuted? For in that case the offence caused by the cross would have been abolished.' (Gal. 5:1-11)

The work of liberation from whatever afflicts us has already been accomplished. He has already set us free. By faith we appropriate what He has already done. So we do not pray in ways that suggest that He needs to do what He has already done! The one who exercises faith is appropriating the finished work of Christ, what He has already accomplished.

He who lives within you has completed all He needed to do for your salvation and healing. He is now seated in triumph with His Father in heaven because He has successfully completed all He was sent to do! There is nothing left for Him to do until He comes again in Majesty and Glory!

Meanwhile He lives in those who believe in Him to continue to outwork His purposes here on earth through them.

Jesus spent much of His time healing the sick. This was one way of demonstrating that the sovereign reign of His Kingdom was within reach of all who turned to Him! And His commission to His church is to preach the gospel of God's Kingdom and to heal the sick. With Christ in us both are possible!

Receiving healing

Most Christians are either in need of some kind of healing themselves, or need to pray for people who are sick. If Christ is in you, then the Healer is within you. You are not praying to a distant God who is not involved in your situation.

I have been involved in the healing ministry for over forty years and have seen thousands healed by Christ from minor ailments to life-threatening diseases for which there has been no medical cure. But I have also seen many pray for healing but without receiving.

Some would suggest, as Jesus does, that faith is the most important element of prayer. After all, He said: "*I tell you this truth most emphatically, if you have faith and do not doubt the outcome, you can not only do similar things to this, but you can also command this mountain, 'Go, throw yourself into the sea,' and it will be moved. You see, no matter what you ask in prayer you will receive if you truly believe.*" (Matt. 21:22)

That seems comprehensive, but raises the question as to what Jesus means by His word 'believe.'

If you believe the answer to your prayer is in the future, it will always be in the future and will never arrive. People can say: "I believe God will heal me." Strictly speaking that is not faith, but hope. Faith is concerned with the present, hope with the future.

If the healer is within you then potentially, at the very least, your healing is within you. Could it be that people are praying to God in heaven to do something in the future, when all the time Christ the Healer who lives in them wants to release His healing power within them in the present?

If Christ is in me I can receive His healing grace at any time anywhere. I do not even need to receive ministry from anyone else. By faith I can appropriate the healing life and power of Christ within me, made available to me through the cross. Now this opens up some exciting possibilities!

I can draw on His power and receive healing whenever I exercise faith in Him. His life and power are in His words. **So I can take the eternal words of Christ, speak them prayerfully over my life and expect the power to be released in my body or the circumstances for which I pray.** Because Christ is in me, He must want to see the release of His power in my body or circumstances!

I have received much healing myself in this way, both by instantaneous miraculous power, and in a more gradual way over as period of time. And I have taught many others to do likewise.

Prayer for healing is not intended to be a kind of spiritual lottery where we pray and wait to see what happens. *'True faith is being sure of the hope we have and being certain that we shall see what has been promised, even though we do not see these things at present'* (Heb. 11:1). It is not a lottery: it is being 'sure' and 'certain'! So believe that Christ is in you, the Healer is in you, your healing is in you. In the great prophecy about the crucifixion we read:

> *'Surely he took up our infirmities and carried our sorrows, yet we considered him stricken by God, smitten by him, and afflicted. But he was pierced for our transgressions, he was crushed for our iniquities; the punishment that brought us peace was upon him, and by his wounds we are healed.'*
> *(Isaiah 53:4-5 NIV)*

Although written some 700 years before the event, the prophet spoke of what was accomplished when Christ was crucified. Certainly the cross is now the most famous event in history, and God has done all that He intended to do through the sacrifice of His Son. He has taken our infirmities upon Himself. He has suffered the punishment for our sin and disobedience, so that now we can be at peace with God. And by His wounds we are healed. Not shall be healed, for that healing has taken place!

The Christ that accomplished that healing is now within you by His Spirit and will give life to your mortal body, as Paul says. What is more, He will flow with healing power into those for whom you pray. You need to believe this, for the Lord honours such faith.

Bold faith

The tentative disciples of the gospels became the new men of bold faith after they had received the Holy Spirit, once the Christ who was with them had come to live in them!

In the unfolding revelation that Jesus gave His disciples things reached a climax with all He said to them at the Last Supper, as recorded in John's gospel. The key statement Jesus made must have sounded like a truly revolutionary statement to these men.

> 'Stay living in Me and I will continue to live in you. It is impossible for any branch to be fruitful if it is separated from the Vine. It has to continue to live in the Vine. In the same way it would be impossible for you to bear fruit if you were not to remain living in Me.' (John 15:4)

To translate this literally we would say: 'Continue to live in me and I continue to live in you!' There is a tense in Greek that denotes continual present action. The Father has placed us in Christ and Christ into us. But we are given the privilege of being put into Christ and the privilege of having Christ put into us. Therefore we have the responsibility to continue to live in Him. Then He will continue to live in us.

It is wonderful that Jesus Christ is with us always. It is even more wonderful that He continues to live in us. This truth transformed these first disciples. Peter and John spoke and acted with authority when they healed the crippled beggar at the Beautiful Gate to the temple:

> 'Both looked directly at him and Peter said: "Look us in the eye!" The man did so, expecting to receive something from them.
>
> Peter said to him: "I don't have any silver or gold to give you, but what I do have I give you now. Walk, in the name of Jesus Christ of Nazareth."' (Acts 3:4-6)

This healing created quite a stir and the two disciples addressed the crowd that gathered:

> 'People of Israel, why does this amaze you? Why look at us as if we have caused this man to walk by some power of our own or by our godliness? Your God, the God of Abraham,

Isaac and Jacob, has glorified His servant Jesus through this miracle. You handed Him over to the Roman authorities to be crucified and rejected Him before Pilate, even though he wanted to release Him. You denied the Holy and Righteous One and demanded that a terrorist murderer be released instead. You were responsible for putting to death the One who gave you life. Yet God raised Him from the dead and we are witnesses of His resurrection.

So by faith in the person of Jesus this man has been healed, and he is someone you clearly recognise. It is by the name of Jesus and the faith that comes from knowing Him, that this complete healing has been given to this man, as you can all see clearly for yourselves.' (Acts 3:12-16)

With Jesus Christ alive in you and because you live in Him, such bold faith can be yours. After all, Jesus Christ is the Author and Perfecter of our faith (Heb. 12:2). So the One within you wants to encourage you to exercise such faith. **You have the authority to act in the name of Jesus. You have the faith He has given you. You have the power of the Holy Spirit that can operate through you.**

A member of the church to which I belong was amazed at how God used her when she trusted Him to do so. In testifying to some of the things she had seen God do through her she said, **"You never know what you have within you until you give it away!"** How true! Many believers have never trusted the Christ within them to work powerfully through them. It is not a matter of praying for more power but of using the power of the risen Christ within you so that He might use you!

Later Peter and John were present when the believers met together to pray: *"Stretch out your hand to heal and perform miraculous signs and wonders through the name of your holy servant Jesus."* (Acts 4:30) We would all say "Amen" to that prayer. But how does He answer such a prayer? By working through these in whom He lives, who are ready to step out with bold faith!

You may feel tentative when you first act in His name, but your confidence will grow and your faith will become bolder as you appreciate that, 'It is not I, but Christ in me', doing His work through me. Certainly, the Holy Spirit within you will encourage you, for you do not know what you have within you until you give it away!

Relationship with Jesus

In John's Gospel we are given privileged insight into the relationship Jesus had with the Father during His ministry on earth. What John wants his readers to appreciate is that we can relate to Jesus now in the same way that He related to the Father then.

We can speak words that Jesus gives us to speak, just as Jesus only spoke the words His Father gave Him to speak. We can do the things we see Jesus doing, as He did only what He saw His Father doing. Apart from Jesus we can do nothing, as Jesus could do nothing apart from His Father. All things are possible for us through faith in Jesus, just as all things were possible for Jesus because of His unity with the Father. We need to dare to believe what Jesus says we can do because we believe in Him:

> *'I will not leave you alone; I will come to you. Soon the world will not be able to see Me any longer, but you will see Me. Because I live, you will also live filled with My life.'*
> *(John 14:19)*

What happened when Jesus returned to the Father? The Spirit of Christ came to the believers and radically altered their lives, making them men and women with bold faith who acted powerfully in the Name of Jesus!

It is a matter of daring to believe that you can do the same things as Jesus because Christ now lives in you!

Greater things still? Yes, for you can pray with others for the Holy Spirit to fill their lives, something Jesus did not do in His ministry because when He spoke of streams of living water pouring out from within believers Jesus *'was referring to the Holy Spirit. Later those who believed in Him would be filled with God's Spirit. Until then, His Spirit had not been given to live within anyone. This would not happen until Jesus had returned to heaven in glory!'* (John7:39) Now He is glorified. Now He lives in you to work through you, the Spirit of the risen, ascended, victorious and glorified Christ!

We have seen that He not only will work through you in mighty ways, but in a thousand different ways, producing more olives on your tree! But you still need bold faith to see God work in all those minor ways as well. It is a matter of thinking spiritually, supernaturally, about every situation that confronts you. Remember, you have your natural mind, but you also have the mind of Christ because He lives within you. And the Holy Spirit will lead you, showing you what to believe in every situation.

So do not put faith in your doubts or your fearful feelings! **Put your trust in the living Christ, in His Word and in the enabling of the Holy Spirit who lives in you.**

Faith is a choice. It is not true to say that you do not have sufficient faith. God's grace works in our lives in such a way that He always makes available whatever faith we need to meet the situation before us. It is a matter of whether we choose to believe our natural thoughts or feelings, or whether we believe God's Word and His promises. You have the choice. **God wants you to take the faith option on every occasion!**

I often say to young couples when they marry, "There will be many times in your life together when you can take the natural option which will seem the safe one, or the faith option that will be the right one!"

Many church leaders want to take safe options, thus depriving themselves and their congregations of the release of power that could take place if they only took the faith options.

Because Jesus Christ is the author of faith, it is obvious which option He encourages, He wants to see our trust in Him growing ever stronger! When we take the safe option we are depending on ourselves. When we take the faith option we are trusting in Christ who lives in us!

However, He is not only the Author of our faith; He is also our Wisdom from God. Faith takes us beyond reason, but God does not encourage us to be foolish or presumptuous in the way we act. We are actually guilty of doing that when we take the initiative out of God's hands.

We have seen that in everything He did, Jesus trusted in His Father; He did not take the initiative out of His Father's hands. He was doing His Father's will, doing what He first saw His Father doing. In other words the Father told Jesus what to believe.

Jesus will do the same for you. **He will tell you what to believe and will show you what you are to do.**

Things begin to go wrong as soon as we take the initiative out of God's hands. Let me give you some examples so you can understand the difference between faith and presumption.

When believing God to provide the necessary finance to purchase the buildings we now use for Kingdom Faith College, the Lord said to me: 'Colin, I give you a million dollars.' That was His initiative. In due course the million dollars arrived and we were able to complete the purchase.

From the moment Jesus spoke that word to me I believed in my heart I had that million dollars, even though at the time nothing happened to demonstrate this.

However, if I had said, "Lord, I am believing you for a million dollars," that would have been my initiative, and would therefore have been presumption. I would be telling God what to do, rather than responding to His initiative.

On another occasion the Lord told me to go and order a new car that was needed for our ministry and He promised to supply the finance for it. I obeyed and ordered the car, although I had no money to pay for it at that time. In His faithfulness to His promise, God supplied the money (without me telling anyone about the need!) before the delivery date for the car. The money was not manipulated by dropping hints to other people about the need! The initiative was with God; He told me to go and order the car.

However, one of the young men in the ministry team thought, "If God can do that for Colin He can do it for me.' So He went out and ordered a new car for himself. But this was his own initiative, and so the money did not arrive and he had to ask to be released from the sale contract!

Faith comes from hearing God, not from telling Him what to do!

When ministering to others in need it is important to keep listening to God. So we know how to pray and act. The Christ in us is to retain the initiative. We are not taking that from Him and telling Him what to do.

In the early years of my ministry, when I began to see many healing miracles, I learned not to pray with everyone in the same way, but to be sensitive to the Spirit on each occasion. It was like saying, "How should I pray with this person?" "What should I do on this occasion?"

In the gospels we see Jesus healing people in many different ways. Even the same condition, such as blindness, was healed in different ways on different occasions. Presumably He was doing what the Father told Him to do.

So with us, we are to do what the Spirit of Christ within us is telling us to do. If we obey Him we will always see the right results, for **the Spirit will never lead us to do what will not work.** But when we take the initiative into our own hands then we will not obtain the same results.

The crippled beggar that Peter and John healed in Jesus' Name was carried to the temple gate every day, the scripture tells us. So Jesus would have walked past Him on a number of occasions, but never healed him. Because the disciples went daily to the temple to pray, they must have walked past him on numerous occasions.

So why was this occasion different? The Spirit of Christ within them must have stirred them to action on this particular day.

I have experienced the Lord saying such things to me when I would not have thought the circumstances right. But by obeying the Spirit, His miraculous power was released. It is really a matter of learning to do what you are told to do by the Spirit. If you learn to do that, you will discover that you do not need to take the initiative away from God and into our own hands. His timing is always perfect and He will always tell you what to do.

However, you do have to make yourself available to the Lord, to be ready to respond to the opportunities that arise. It is a matter of understanding that when they arise, you proceed by listening to the Lord directing you, even giving you the words to speak or to pray!

So you are always ready to pray for the sick, unless you sense the Spirit saying that it is not the right time to do so with that particular person. However, when you pray you want the Spirit of Christ to lead you, so that you pray in the way that will be most effective. Like Jesus, you are doing what you see to be right in that particular situation.

Jesus' ability to reveal the Father through what He said and did came out of His relationship with the Father. The same will be true of us; **our ability to reveal Christ through what we say and do will come out of our relationship with Him.** Prayer builds and strengthens that relationship and enables us to become sensitive to the voice of His Spirit.

A good part of our prayer time needs to be spent in listening to the Lord, through God's Word and by His Spirit. A good practice is to take a portion of scripture and write down in your prayer journal what God is saying to you through those verses. As you come into tune with His Spirit in this way, He will speak to you also of issues that concern you, for He is aware of all the circumstances you face and what you need to hear from Him, so that you can fulfil His will for you.

If you require an answer from the Lord about a certain matter, do not strain to hear the answer from Him. Lay the matter before Him and leave it with Him. When you least expect it, He will then speak to you about that matter at a time when you are not even thinking about that particular situation. This will help you to have confidence that you have heard the voice of the Spirit instead of listening to your own thoughts and understanding.

Christ in you wants to lead you in the way you are to go, to fulfil the plans He has for you. Being yielded to Him makes this a simple matter. Things only become complicated and difficult when we fight against the Lord and do not want to submit to His authority! When we are self-willed and independent!

When our hearts are submitted to Him, it is not difficult to hear what He is saying, for the Spirit of Christ within you is not silent. He has not suddenly become dumb! In fact He is speaking to you more than you probably realise, which is why you need to spend time listening to Him.

Time spent listening in prayer enables you to hear the voice of His Spirit in the middle of the activity of your daily life. If you start the day by tuning into His voice you can stay tuned in for the rest of the day! It is like turning your radio to a particular station. Once tuned in you can switch the radio set on at any time and you are tuned into the right station!

Christ is your righteousness and holiness. So walking in loving obedience to Him helps the whole process of being able to hear clearly what He is saying. Sin cuts across your relationship with the Lord, and this can make it difficult to hear clearly until you have repented in a suitable way. Then by His mercy the relationship is restored and you can again walk closely with Him; you in Christ and Christ in you!

Nothing can take precedence in your life over your relationship with Jesus Christ. This has to come first, just as Jesus never allowed anything to interfere with His relationship with His Father. If He was kept busy during the day by the constant crowds of people wanting Him to minister to them, He would spend the night in prayer.

The person who says, 'I am too busy to pray' needs to reassess his or her priorities. And it is not good to leave times of prayer to the end of the day when we are so tired that we fall asleep!

Even mothers with small children can find time to pray, although that may not be possible first thing in the morning. Business men will prosper if Jesus has His rightful place in prayer. Tuning in with God enables busy people to stay tuned in during the hectic schedule that they have. **If you have the right priorities, Christ will have His rightful place – on the throne of your life, the most important place!**

CHAPTER 10

HE IS YOUR VICTORY

Throughout this book I have referred to the fact that Christ is our victory; He enables us to overcome, to conquer and be victorious! We have seen that God always leads us in His triumphant procession in Christ; that He has overcome enemy adversity on the cross, enabling us to be in that triumphant procession.

We have seen that if we do not fight in our own strength, He will fight for us! It is not by our own might or power, but by the Spirit of Christ within us that we shall prevail! So now we need to see how to allow Christ to be our victory in the daily circumstances of our lives; how to allow Him to give us the victory. Remember the principle:

> I cannot, but He can.
>
> If I do not, He will.
>
> If I do, He will not.

Who is in the driving seat and who is the passenger? Are you going to be in the driving seat and relegate Jesus to be the passenger? Or are you going to move over so that He can be in the driving seat and you the passenger, allowing Him to take you wherever He wants to lead you?

Are you ready to stop fighting and striving to advance in your own strength? This is the problem for many, especially those driven by an inner need to be successful, to be seen as achievers! Is your identity in your ability to accomplish, or in Christ? Are you a driven person, or one who is led by His Spirit? Are you fighting to maintain your old identity or willing to discover your new identity in Christ?

These are significant questions because your answers to them will determine how fully you will apply the teaching of this book; or rather, how fully you will live in the revelation that Christ is in you, the hope of glory!

Compromise is an enemy of the truth and it would be easy to settle for a partnership: some of Christ and some of you! In fact, this is the compromise that many believers adopt. The truth is: 'Not I, but Christ in me!' That is very different from, 'I and Christ' or even, 'Christ and I.'

The self part of this partnership will always be the weak and vulnerable part. It is an assumption that Christ would even agree to such a partnership! Does He really want to be limited in your life by such a compromise? Paul discovered the truth as we saw at the beginning of this study:

> *'I have been crucified together with Christ; the person I was no longer lives, but Christ now lives in me. The life I live in my body I live by faith in God's Son, who has loved me by giving Himself on my behalf.' (Gal. 2:20).*

Does compromise mean that you are now asking Christ to partner with one who no longer lives? Or to partner with the natural self life that Jesus says you are to deny daily. It does not seem to make much sense to say in effect: "Thank you, Lord, for coming to live in me. But I do not want you to take over; I want you to partner with my self-life about which you say there is nothing good!"

The nature of your heart will determine how fully you are prepared to surrender to the authority of Christ in you!

The nature of the problem

The problem lies in our desire to please ourselves, or to order our affairs according to our own preferences. We tend to do this even about spiritual things. For example, we want the church to which we belong to have the kind of worship we enjoy (although worship is for God's glory, not to fulfil our desires!), the form of service that is neither too long nor too short, the kind of preaching with which we agree, that encourages but is not too challenging or demanding. We may not want to become involved with other church members, even though we are to love them as Christ loves us. We may feel it right to be critical of the leadership if they came to decisions with which we do not agree. And so on.

You can see how much of self is in such attitudes. Certainly they do not reflect the denying of ourselves, but they give the impression that the church exists to please us rather than please the Lord! It raises the question: 'Who is the Head of the Church?' We all know the right answer: Jesus Christ. **But is He allowed to be the Head if His people have so many preferences.**

And how can there be the unity among believers for which Jesus prayed, when within a single congregation there can be so many different preferences, with people fighting for their desires to win the day and their opinions to be accepted by the congregation. What kind of a witness is this to unbelievers? Contrast this with Jesus prayer for all those who will become believers in Him:

> *'I pray that they will be one in faith and love, Father, in the same way that you and I are always in complete harmony and agreement: you in Me and I in you. May they continue to live in us so that the world will believe who I AM, the One you sent to be their Saviour and Lord.' (John 17:21-23)*

As Jesus prayed these words, we can be sure they are His will for us as His church. So we look at each objective for which He prays:

- As we have seen, believers are in both the Father and the Son.
- Demonstrating our unity with the Lord will prove to the world that Jesus Christ is God's Son.
- Jesus has given to believers His glory, for His glorified Spirit now lives in them, to reveal His glory to the world.
- There is to be a unity of relationship between believers that reflects the unity between the Father and the Son. We are not to be divided by our own personal preferences and agendas.
- Our unity will not only reveal that Jesus Christ is God's Son; it will also show that the Father loves us in the same way that He loved Jesus.

This raises the question as to how the Father loved Jesus:

> *'My Father loves Me because I am ready to die for the sheep, only then to be restored to life.' (John 10:17)*

So we are called to lay down our lives so that the world might believe: 'Not I, but Christ in me!' Jesus lived, not to do His own will, but the will of the Father who sent Him!

Jesus prayed for the right relationships, that He would be in us in the same way that the Father had been working in and through Him. This part of His prayer has already been fulfilled; for Jesus is already in us as the risen, glorified Christ.

What does He intend us to be therefore? **A body of people in whom He lives, who are no longer living for themselves. They have died to their preferences and their own agendas and opinions. They live to reveal Christ in their lives, so He can be revealed in and through each member of the Body of Christ.**

Imagine what the effect and influence would be if an entire congregation lived in such a way. For Christ is not only to be revealed through the individual members of His Body, but through the Body as a whole, the Body of which He is the Head.

Actually, it is impossible to imagine, for to our shame no such church exists. Instead the church is full of spots and wrinkles, the imperfections that mar the revelation of the risen Christ we are to give to the world. Is there anything to be done about this state of affairs, or do we simply accept church as we know it and continue in ways that are familiar and usually comfortable?

What would be involved if God was to revive His church? He would bring His people back to the truth of His Word, back to a total dependence on Him and a denying of ourselves so that we could live as true disciples of Jesus Christ!

Such a revival can at least begin in you, as you apply the teaching of God's Word to your own life. You will then have a personal revival, and a revival will at least have begun in your congregation! You do not have to wait for anyone to lead you into a revival. Here and now it can begin by you saying with Paul:

> *'I have been crucified together with Christ; the person I was*
> *no longer lives, but Christ now lives in me. The life I live*
> *in my body I live by faith in God's Son who has loved me by*
> *giving Himself on my behalf.' (Gal. 2:20)*

Make these words your own: 'Not I, but Christ in me!'

Be thankful that your own weakness no longer matters, for God's grace is sufficient for you, and His power is made perfect in your weakness! **Know that you are embarking on a wonderful adventure, seeing what Christ in you will do through you! You will see how He can give you the victory and enable you to overcome, conquer and be victorious because you give way to the victorious one within you.**

As you take this decision to live in the way that God intends you to live, do not be discouraged if you find the self-life intruding again and again. This happens at the beginning of the process, for God's Spirit has to show us the many different ways in which we have depended on ourselves instead of on Christ in us. The realisation of how much self-dependence there is in your life can shock you! Do not be discouraged, neither give up. Paul said of Jesus:

> *'He only needed to die once, and when He did so He dealt with the power of sin once and for all. Now He lives to reveal the truth of God and His amazing grace.' (Rom. 6:10)*

The apostle then urges his readers to die to sin in a similar way:

> *'In a similar way, realise that you can consider yourself to have died to sin, but that you are now raised to an entirely new life that you can enjoy through your unity with Christ as you live for God's glory!' (Rom. 6:11)*

In a similar way, realise that you can consider yourself to have died to sin, but that you are now raised to an entirely new life that you can enjoy through your unity with Christ as you live for God's glory!

Do not wait for some experience to indicate that you have died to that sinful self. Count and reckon yourself dead because you have been crucified with Christ. That self-life need not dominate your life any longer. Today you can deny yourself and take up your cross to follow Christ.

> *'When you died with Christ you died to the law; now you are united with Him in His risen life.' (Rom. 7:6)*

Now the will of God is written on our hearts, and because of our love for him we desire to please Him by obeying His commands. And we appreciate that the only way this is possible is through the life and power of the risen Christ within us. 'Not I, but Christ in me!'

CHAPTER 11

YOUR WALK IN THE TRUTH

Your relationship with God is described in scripture as a walk with Him. This implies movement; it is not something static! You are going places with God! But you are not going alone, for Christ is in you! You walk in obedience to His commands because you love Him.

> *'As you have heard, His concern is that we walk in love.'*
> *(2 John 6)*

It is a walk in the truth:

> *'It gave me great joy when some brothers came and testified that you live in the truth, and told of how you continue to walk in the truth. There can be no greater joy for me than to hear of my spiritual children walking in the truth.' (3 John 4)*

It is a walk in the light of the revelation that Jesus is the light of life:

> *'If we claim to share in His Light and yet walk in spiritual darkness, we only lie and do not live according to the truth. But, if we walk in the Light just as He is in the Light, we share in His Life together and the blood of Jesus, His Son, purifies us from all sin, from everything we have done against His will.' (1 John 1:6-7)*

And Jesus promised

> *'Then Jesus addressed the crowd again and said: "I, I AM the Light of the world. Anyone who follows me will never*

walk in spiritual darkness because he has the life that gives
him light.' (John 8:12)

The walk even turns into a run! And we are to run to win the prize!

'In a race everyone competes but only one wins the trophy
for coming first. You know this well. Run as if you are
determined to win that trophy. Every competitor has to
go into strict training if he expects to win the crown, even
though such an honour has no lasting value. But we run to
receive a crown of eternal significance.' (1 Cor. 9:24-25)

We can rejoice that Christ is in us, to enable us to finish the race and
obtain the crown. We want to be able to say like Paul:

'I have fought the good fight, I have finished the course
God had for me and I have been faithful. Now the crown
of righteousness awaits me, which the Lord, the righteous
Judge, will award to me on that Day; and not only to me,
but also to all who have longed for His appearing.' (2 Tim.
4:7-8)

How wonderful, then, that Christ Himself is your righteousness, that the
walk does not depend on any righteousness of your own. It is as well that He
is your holiness.

'So do all you can to ensure that you live at peace with
others. And be holy; live as one whom God has set apart for
Himself. For without holiness no one will see the Lord and
belong to Him eternally.' (Heb. 12:14)

You can rejoice that He is your life and your victory. As you trust Him He
will give you the victory, enabling you to overcome, to conquer, to be victorious and so receive the crown of life.

This is the wonderful truth that the New Testament proclaims. What the law of God could never achieve because of our human weakness, Christ Jesus has now accomplished through obedience to the Father, and then by offering Himself in sacrifice for us. He is now the risen, ascended, glorified Christ reigning in heaven.

Yet the exalted Christ also lives in you and me and in every believer. The One who has overcome lives in you so that by trusting Him you will overcome and receive the crown of eternal life.

What wonderful good news! Live in the good of this revelation that you have been crucified with Christ. It is no longer you who live but Christ lives in you. The life you now live here on earth you live by faith in the One who died for you because of His great love for you, and now lives in you to reign through your life as the King of Kings and the Lord of Lords!

APPENDIX 1:
RELEVANT SCRIPTURES

There follows a number of scriptures that are particularly relevant for living in the good of 'The Great Revelation.'

As part of your daily prayer time it would be good to take a number of these and receive the life that God wants to communicate to you through His Word. Repeat each scripture a few times either aloud or quietly to yourself, knowing that God is speaking His Truth into your heart. I have gained much from using the scriptures in this way for many years.

Occasionally you will benefit from reading through all these verses at one time. Do this prayerfully and you will be full of praise and thanks to God for all that He has done for us and has given you.

Through God's work of grace you now live in Christ Jesus, at one with Him. (1 Cor. 1:30)

Because you live in Christ you have been blessed with all His riches. (1 Cor. 1:5)

For this reason you do not lack any of His Spiritual gifts. (1 Cor. 1:7)

Stay living in Me and I will continue to live in you. (John. 15:4)

I have been crucified together with Christ; the person I was no longer lives, but now Christ lives in me. (Gal. 2:20)

The life I live in my body I live by faith in God's Son, who has loved me by giving Himself on my behalf. (Gal. 2:20)

Because you died with Christ, your life is now hidden with Christ – in God! (Col. 3:3)

He is our righteousness.   He is our holiness.   He is our redemption. (1 Cor. 1:30)

Christ has now come to live in you, and in Him alone is your hope of glory. (Col. 1:27)

Be united with Me and learn from Me, for I have a humble and gentle heart; then you will find peace for your souls. (Matt. 11:29)

My grace is always sufficient to meet your need. My power is revealed more perfectly through your weakness. (2 Cor. 12:8)

He has blessed us through our life in Christ with every spiritual blessing that belongs to the heavenly Kingdom. (Eph. 1:3)

God's Kingdom is within you. (Luke 17:21)

We share in the life of the Father and of His Son Jesus Christ. (1 John 1:3)

For all of you are made sons of God through faith in Christ Jesus. (Gal 3:26)

Everything that the Father has, I also have. And everything I have the Spirit will take and reveal to you in your experience. (John 16:15)

My son, you are always with Me and everything that is Mine is yours. (Luke 15:31)

I will never leave you, nor forsake you. (John 1:8)

I have loved you in exactly the same way that My Father loves Me. So continue to live in My love. (John 15:9)

Anyone who genuinely loves Me will be loved by My Father. I will also love him and will continue to reveal Myself to him. (John 14:21)

Remain faithful and I will give you the crown of life. (Rev. 2:10)

Trust in the Lord with all your heart and do not depend on your own understanding. (Prov. 3:5)

Let the Word of Christ live in you in all its richness. (Col. 3:16)

The words I have spoken to you contain the life of God's Spirit. (John 6:63)

When you believe, everything becomes possible. (Mark 9:23)

No matter what you ask in prayer you will receive if you truly believe. (Matt. 21:22)

You have authority to prevent on earth what heaven does not allow, and you can release on earth what has been released from heaven. (Matt. 18:18)

If you had true faith…nothing would be impossible for you. (Matt. 17:21)

I will give you whatever you ask in My Name and in this way the Son will bring further glory to the Father. (John 14:13)

So I tell you, no matter what you ask in prayer, believe it is already yours and it will be yours. (Mark 11:24)

Be sure that no matter what you say or do, you are able to do everything in the name of Jesus. (Col. 3:17)

Father, I thank You that You have heard Me and I know that You always hear Me. (John 11:41-42)

Certainly it will be as I have planned; and My purposes will stand. (Is. 14:24)

All those who have been baptised into Christ have been clothed with Christ. (Gal. 3:27)

Walk in the ways My Spirit leads you, and you will not gratify what your self-life desires! (Col. 5:16)

I have given you authority to overcome every power the enemy has. Nothing will be able to harm you as you exercise that authority. (Luke 10:19)

Obey My commands from your heart, for they will prolong your life and will cause you to prosper. (Prov. 3:1-2)

The Lord poured His grace abundantly upon Me, together with the faith and love that are in Christ Jesus. (1 Tim. 1:14)

God's peace be upon you. I am now sending you, just as the Father has sent Me. (John 20:21)

But thanks be to God, for He always leads us in triumphant procession because we are in Christ. (2 Cor. 2:14)

I am like an olive tree flourishing in the house of God; I trust in His unfailing love for ever and ever. (Ps. 52:8)

He will keep you strong to the very end so that on that glorious day when you come before our Lord Jesus Christ, you will be without any blame or guilt. (1 Cor. 1:8)

The glory You gave Me I have given to all who believe in Me that they may be united in faith and love, reflecting the unity between us as Father and Son. (John 17:22)

I will return for you to ensure that you will be with Me eternally in My heavenly glory. (John 14:3)

APPENDIX 2:
'THE TRUTH' VERSION

There follows a quotation from the Introduction to 'The Truth'. The New Testament easily understood:

The task of producing another English version of the New Testament is not something I would have undertaken without a keen sense from the Holy Spirit that this was what God wanted me to do. Certainly, I have never had any personal desire for such a task.

It has proved to be a very rewarding experience for me personally. Having been a preacher and teacher of God's Word for over 45 years I have a great love for the scriptures and I have been devoted to bringing understanding of its significance for modern living to people in over 40 nations, where I have had the privilege of ministering in the name of Jesus Christ.

As someone who has been interpreted into several languages I am familiar with the process of translating the meaning of the truth from one language to another. I have been blessed with many wonderful interpreters over the years. They have impressed on me that the best interpreters do not necessarily translate what I say literally, but express what I say in a way that will be understood clearly in their own language.

As the principle of a Bible College, among several other aspects of ministry, I have always been deeply concerned that any version of the New Testament should be accurate. But I have also been acutely aware that people will only translate God's Word into action in their lives if they clearly understand its meaning and implications for them personally.

I mentioned these things so that you can understand the principles behind this particular version, 'The Truth'. Any translation inevitably involves a certain amount of interpretation. There are two types of translation available today. Some are strict word by word or phrase by phrase translations. These are accurate translations of the original Greek text, but do not necessarily draw out the meaning of the text.

On the other extreme are modern paraphrases which are certainly edifying but often seem to depart from the original. I believe that God wanted me to chart a middle course between these two extremes.

I sought to do this by first translating the text literally, and then asking the questions, 'What does this mean? How would you express this in today's world, with the modern mindset that people have?'

It seemed an awesome task to maintain accuracy with the Greek text and yet have the freedom to expand the translation where necessary so that it can be readily understood. This I have done by sometimes giving the literal translation of the Greek followed by another phrase that puts the same truth in another way that can be readily appreciated by the reader.

I sensed the Lord encouraging me in this by reminding me frequently that this exactly what a good preacher does. He reads the Word and explains it. Yet this had to be done without turning this edition into either a commentary or a study Bible! The text needed to be easily readable and readily understood.

KINGDOM FAITH

Kingdom Faith is a multi-faceted ministry that originally formed around the apostolic ministry of Colin Urquhart. For over thirty years, Kingdom Faith has enjoyed a continual move of the Holy Spirit, including periods of genuine revival that have had a wide impact far beyond the ministry itself.

The many books written by Colin Urquhart express the emphases and life-style of Kingdom Faith, faith in God's Word and obedience to the leading of the Holy Spirit. The main focus is on the Kingdom of God, where Jesus placed the emphasis during His ministry. The revivals experienced have been based on key elements of the Kingdom that God wants to see reproduced in the whole of His church: love, faith and holiness.

This is the life-style that results from the corporate anointing now upon Kingdom Faith and that is expressed in the various aspects of its ministry, which are:

Kingdom Faith Church:

The main apostolic congregation meets in the National Revival Centre in Horsham, West Sussex, with Clive Urquhart as the Senior Pastor. This is a church intent on reaching the world locally, nationally and internationally, with the gospel of Jesus Christ. This is an exciting church to be part of and has the benefit of a strong leadership team working together in unity. The church has many different evangelistic and compassion ministries.

Kingdom Faith has planted other congregations in Britain and many other churches in Britain and overseas are in covenant relationship with Kingdom Faith. Through this covenant, Kingdom Faith seeks to serve and encourage these churches in the same biblical principles on which Kingdom Faith is based, God's Word and Spirit working together in the lives of individual believers and of the church corporately.

Kingdom Faith Training College:

For over twenty-five years, students from Britain and many other nations from around the world have been trained at this college for a variety of ministries in the Body of Christ. Some students have been used to bring revival to their nations. People have literally come from the nations and have been sent by God to the nations!

Being predominantly a residential college, students are personally discipled to live what they are taught. A strong move of the Spirit takes place in the college every year, reflecting Kingdom Faith's experience of revival. The lives of students are radically transformed by the relationships they develop with the Lord. The college is blessed by enjoying the anointing of God's presence in its worship, teaching and outreach.

Faith Camp:

This annual camp has taken place for over twenty-five years and attracts over 6,000 participants of all ages. These weeks of teaching and ministry are renowned for the ways in which people meet with God through the strong anointing on the worship that Kingdom Faith enjoys, and the way the power of the Holy Spirit impacts their lives.

Several churches bring sizeable groups because of the impact that results on the whole of their congregational life. In one week the church can move on significantly with God in a way that would not otherwise have been possible. Hundreds of people come from other nations as well as from all over Britain. They expect to meet with God, even in miraculous ways.

Covenant relationships:

Many individual believers choose to be in covenant relationship with Kingdom Faith. They support the work in prayer and through giving financially because they identify with the vision of Kingdom Faith. They continue to benefit from the ministry through leadership and general conferences, through times of personal revival and through the wealth of teaching materials that can be accessed from the Kingdom Faith website.

Kingdomfaith.com:

Through this award-winning website you can not only receive more information about the church, college and Faith Camp; you can also share in the life of Kingdom Faith. Thousands watch the live streaming of the Sunday morning services as well as other notable events. Teaching and training materials are also available, mostly free of charge. A weekly keynote message, usually given by Colin Urquhart can also be downloaded.

It is also possible to receive the radio programmes of Colin Urquhart's teaching on the internet, and details of these programmes can be found on www.kingdomfaith.com.

There are also details of various publications available, including how you can obtain copies of 'The Truth', the New Testament in a version easily understood and used in this book.

The purpose of Kingdom Faith:

All connected with Kingdom Faith are devoted to serving the Lord faithfully in fulfilling the commission He has given us to see His Kingdom come and His will done on earth as in heaven. This they do by seeking to live the gospel, knowing their dependence on the Lord, but aware that He lives in them to work through them for His honour and glory. They are aware that it is of vital importance to honour the Lord in all things!

We praise God for His infinite mercy and grace that enables us and we pray that we will remain faithful in fulfilling His call on our lives.